Bill & Hillary's 12-Step Guide to Recovery

—How to Recover

from Anything

iBooks
Habent Sua Fata Libelli

iBooks
1230 Park Avenue
New York, New York 10128
Tel: 212-427-7139
bricktower@aol.com • www.ibooksinc.com

All rights reserved under the International and Pan-American Copyright Conventions.
Printed in the United States by J. Boylston & Company, Publishers, New York.
No part of this publication may be reproduced, stored in a retrieval system, or transmitted in any form or by any means, electronic, or otherwise, without the prior written permission of the copyright holder. The iBooks colophon is a trademark of
J. Boylston & Company, Publishers.

Library of Congress Cataloging-in-Publication Data

Eichler, Glenn.
Bill and Hillary's 12-Step Recovery Guide
p. cm.

1. Satire—Political. 2. Humor
Fiction, I. Title.

ISBN-13: 978-1-59687-xxx-x, Trade Paper

November 2014

Bill & Hillary's 12-Step Guide to Recovery

—How to Recover from Anything

Glenn Eichler

Illustrations by
Splitting Image

For Michele

Explain Whitewater to me again

CONTENTS

PREFACE

By, An Enthusiastic, Anonymous
Supporter of
President Bill Clinton*

My Fellow Americans,

Any public figure with a private problem faces a serious choice: Do I fight this battle alone, behind a curtain of secrecy? Or do I make my struggle public, thus educating the American people about a grave condition and simultaneously guaranteeing myself a nice fat book deal?

So it is with President Bill Clinton—and because of his deep commitment to America, he has decided on the latter, more painful path. His illness? A disastrous presidency. His hope for rehabilitation? A Twelve-Step program of his own devising. My job as his Vice President? To do everything in my power to support and encourage him, all the while edging just out of frame when news photographers snap his picture. And also to remember not to walk in front of the White House windows until they get the bulletproof glass in.

This nation owes Bill Clinton an enormous debt. He came to power in an era of uncertainty about America's future. Twelve years of Republican rule had left the country with deep fundamental problems— yet because these problems had not reached crisis proportions, no one had the courage to address them. Then, with a firm and steady hand at the controls of Starship America, Bill Clinton guided her out of this meteor shower of doubt and straight into a black hole of disappointment. Now we are desperate enough to face our problems. Bill Clinton has brought us to that point of desperation. For that, he deserves our thanks.

That is what your President has done for you. Now it is your turn to do something for him. Support him in this period of recovery. Encourage him. If you can, love him. (I do not mean that last one literally. We already have enough problems to deal with in this campaign. If you should happen to meet the President face to face, and he starts to nuzzle you, please rap him once on the nose, sharply, with a rolled-up newspaper.) And, of course, vote for Clinton-Gore in 1996.

In closing, I would like to paraphrase one of America's greatest poets, Walt Whitman, in his elegy to another noble president, Abraham Lincoln. If I may be so presumptuous as to update "Oh Captain! My Captain" for the age of the information superhighway:

> Oh captain! my captain, the ship of state is toss'd
> We've blown the Senate and the House, and even Cuomo lost
> Oh captain! my captain, they flay you on the news
> They talk of your chicanery and taste for white trash flooze
> Oh captain! my captain, outside Bob Dole awaits
> He says you'll get your ass kicked in the '96 debates
> Oh captain! my captain, 'tis plain that strong you're not
> Perhaps you ought to step aside and give the veep a shot.

God bless you, God bless President Bill Clinton, and now let's go out there and win this thing!

Footnote

* I've got nothing to hide. I'd just rather not have my name linked with his in print, okay?

BILL & HILLARY'S 12 STEP RECOVERY GUIDE

A Political Satire

INTRODUCTION

Why this book, at this point in history, during this stage of our— er, my—administration?

Fellow Americans, Mr. Speaker, esteemed members of the Congress and Cabinet ... I write this today in the hope that we may discuss recovery. Recovery. It's a "buzzword," a word that pushes our "hot buttons," a word that instantly conjures up images of illness, fever, medicine. Doctors, nurses, hospitals. Exorbitant inpatient charges, gouging insurance cartels, an intransigent Congress of cowards bowing to politics and lobbyists and refusing to provide universal health care coverage to the very citizens who elected them despite far more cajoling, horse trading, threatening, and begging than any reasonably intelligent and proud man should be expected to endure . . . well, maybe it doesn't conjure up all those images. Maybe I've been working a little too hard. Damn it, where's that herbal tea?

Anyway, recovery. To be more specific, political recovery. I am not going to stand before you today in these pages and pretend the past several months of my presidency have been an unqualified success. Or the first several months, back in 1993. Or the period in-between. But, my fellow Americans, you elected me to do a job. And the job isn't done. And it's not my fault. And I need a break. And that is why I would like to discuss recovery. Political recovery. My political recovery.

I'd like to tell you about something that happened to me recently. It was late at night, very late, but I couldn't sleep. Every time I closed my eyes, I began to see vivid images of everything that ails our Nation, all the wrongs that still need to be righted. I'd open my eyes and, distressed, reach under the bed for another slice of cold anchovy pizza, and then I'd eat that and close my eyes, and the images would become even more upsetting. Pretty soon it dawned on me that conditions were even worse than I'd realized. I was out of pizza. So I got out of bed and, still in my pajamas, went into the Oval Office and began to pace. Presently I was joined by the First Lady, also in her nightclothes; on this particular evening it turned out to be Hillary. "What's wrong, sweetheart?" she asked me. "I'm worried," I replied, "worried sick. When I was running for President, I had a clear vision. I was able to state my beliefs and my intentions with absolute conviction and clarity. And now, here in this vile cesspool of Washington where wrong is right, up is down, yes means no, I ... I ... I've lost my way. I've lost my way," I said to her, tears welling up in my eyes.

"Oh, that again," she said, and went back to bed.

That's when, alone in that room where so much history has been made, I sat down in the chair where Abraham Lincoln and Franklin D. Roosevelt and John F. Kennedy sat and reflected upon my quandary.

I must have dozed off, because the next thing I knew a deep, sonorous voice was calling me. My eyes snapped open.

"Mr. President," said the voice. "Mr. President."

"What . . . who are you?" I gasped.

"Now you call me Mr. President," it said hopefully.

"Mr. President?" I said.

"God, I miss that," said the voice. Then a human shape began to shimmer before me, and before I knew it I was looking at—the spirit? the ghost?—of Richard M. Nixon. He was wearing a dark suit.

"President Nixon?" I said. "But you're dead."

"Maybe so, but I wouldn't mind an ambassadorship," he answered. "Just kidding! No, I've come back from Yorba Linda to give you some advice. It's something we dead presidents do occasionally for our successors. Like a courtesy service.

"Now listen," Nixon continued. "I know this whole presidency thing hasn't worked out the way you hoped it would, and the picture looks kind of bleak right now. But you're like me. You're a fighter. You're a survivor. You're fundamentally amoral. And you can turn things around.

"Your greatest gift is your ability to communicate with the people of our great Nation. Go to the people. Tell them you had a lousy first term, but you know what went wrong and your second term will be all

the better for it. Tell them your presidency is in recovery, explain to them why and how, and invite them to join the process."

"But how . . . where . . ."

The former president's image was beginning to waver and dissolve. "Books always worked for me," he said. "People love owning a book by a president, and they almost never read them."

He was now barely visible. He raised his arms and gave the V for Victory sign with both hands. "I cannot stay," he said. "I want to drop by Kissinger's and haunt him for a while before daybreak. Remember . . . tell the people how you're getting better . . . Also, get that daughter of yours a dog . . ." The rest of his words were lost in the wind. He was gone.

I sat in my chair and thought. Sure, Nixon had pulled one of the greatest comebacks in political history, but did I really want to take the advice of the most thoroughly disgraced president in recent memory?

It was then that a second figure materialized in the room. To be more specific, there were two figures. I didn't recognize one of them, but the one on top was clearly President John F. Kennedy. Sweating, breathless, obviously in some kind of distress, he spoke to me through clenched teeth. "Take . . . Dick's . . . advice . . . ," he squeezed out, "and when you get here, I'll introduce you to Marilyn Monroe." And then, in a twinkle, he and his pretty friend were gone.

And that decided it. Two presidents had reached out to me from beyond the grave, urging me to bring my case to the people. And that, my fellow Americans, is what I have done. This book is a pledge. A commitment. All that stuff I promised back in '92? I'm going to do it. Really, I really mean it, reelect me and this time it's going to happen. I've seen the light, I know what I've been doing wrong, and, working with a White House task force, I have created my own Twelve Steps to Political Recovery so that I, and Hillary, and the Nation, can make this great move forward together. Provided you vote the right way, of course. You sent me to Washington to do a job; this book should illustrate for you the importance of allowing me to finish that job. If it does not, let me put the argument another way: President Gramm. President Gingrich. President D'Amato.

I would just like to point out that in taking the advice of a dead Republican, my husband has once again shown a willingness to work together in a bipartisan effort to reach his goals. I find it ironic that the live Republicans in the House and Senate are more rigid than Mr. Nixon, despite his having undergone rigor mortis. I've often said I'd love to gather up the living, mediocre Republicans in our legislative branch and trade them all for one good stiff one. In fact, I'd trade almost anything for one good stiff one.

Hillary, sweetheart, I'm not sure our Republican friends will take that statement in the spirit of reconciliation in which it is offered.

Sorry, darling, you're right again as usual. What I meant to say is, we look forward to working with the Republican leadership in both houses in a bipartisan effort to pass meaningful legislation that will improve the lives of every American.

I couldn't have put it better myself.

The scum.

The Twelve Steps to,
Political Recovery.

1. We admit that we have become powerless over Congress and we cannot accomplish anything in the first term.

2. We realize that if we are to achieve a second term, we will need help from a Greater Power. Quite a bit of help, actually.

3. We make a decision to turn our will and our lives over to that Power, which we have learned through governing a state in the Bible Belt to call God.

4. We take stock of ourselves unsparingly and take note of our flaws, no matter how tremendously overshadowed they are by our stellar qualities.

5. We tell God everything that's wrong with ourselves, and ask Him how much of it is likely to come out during the campaign.

6. We tell God we're ready to have Him remove all defects of character, and humbly ask His permission to leak the good news.

7. We respectfully ask Him to get it done before the New Hampshire primary.

8. We make a list of political enemies we've made and determine their influence in Congress, the media and the public arena.

9. We kiss up to as many of those people as possible and promise appointments to the rest.

10. We keep making lists of everything wrong with us, on the slim chance that we'll be ready the next time the media unearths something we did in the '80s.

11. We keep trying to get on God's good side. And everyone else's too, except those pricks Gingrich and Dole, who don't have one.

12. We carry our message of redemption and reelection to others through sound bites, photo ops and the occasional interminable speech.

Chapter One

A PLACE CALLED
HOPELESS:

THE ROOTS OF RECOVERY

The beautiful magnolia blossom doesn't spring to life from thin air. It blooms from a bud on a branch, which grows from a tree, which is nourished by roots that burrow deep into the soil. So it is with festering, crippling political problems. They don't just appear out of nowhere one day like a process server with a fistful of sexual harassment suits. No, their origins are to be found in our own histories. That is why I'd like to touch briefly on my own.

According to my mother, my decisiveness problems started before I was born. Arkansas was a conservative state, but my Momma and Daddy were very progressive people. They almost always ate with utensils, for one thing. For another, my Daddy owned one of the only English-language *Kama Sutras* in the South. According to family legend, it was the night Daddy (we never did get his name) put my mother through the first ten chapters, almost killing her, that she finally cried out in exasperation, "For God's sake, would you just pick a position and stay with it!"

Daddy never did settle on one position that night—the night I was conceived—and Mama always said that was the reason I could never settle on one position, either. I've learned not to hate my father for leaving me that legacy; heck, he also left me his *Kama Sutra*, and those Persian babes really knew how to express their respect for their leaders. Our modern network anchormen could learn a thing or two from them.

I still carry that book with me everywhere I go. Sure, it's older now, and the pages are yellowed and scribbled over with my notes and diagrams, but it reminds me of my Daddy and the most valuable lesson he taught me: There is only so much you can learn from a book. Then you've got to just get out there and plunge in.

Bill, darling, if I might interject a thought of my own, I would say that your story contains an even more important lesson for a recovering President. It illustrates a truth about your parents' relationship that you can apply to *your* relationship with Congress: Fancy positions will only take you so far. In the end, what matters is that you screw their brains out.

Why, thank you, Hillary! I see your point and you're absolutely right.

Now what is this about a *Kama Sutra* you take everywhere you go? How come I never heard about it?

Did I forget to mention that?

I'd love to see it, Bill, sweetheart.

Uh, I left it in Tokyo at the economic summit. No, wait, I lent it to Packwood a while back. Yeah, Packwood. I'll call him.

Learning to Listen to the People

Anyway, that's all I know about my conception. I don't really remember much about my birth, either, except really enjoying the trip through the birth canal and vowing to revisit it often. My early years are also pretty much a blur, especially that period at Oxford when I was corresponding with my draft board. I do recall, when I was two, my Momma begging and pleading with me to go in the toilet instead of in my diaper. I saw her point, and felt that she was absolutely right, but at the same time I thought of the diaper manufacturer and the diaper cleaning service, and I feared that if I began using the toilet it might cost American jobs. For the next three years I carefully weighed the consequences of each option; ultimately I decided that it was important to my future and, more importantly, the future of the country, that I go ahead and do poo-poo in the potty.

Those early years in the depressed little town of Hope, Arkansas—well, not *in* Hope exactly, but very nearby in a slightly more depressed little town called Hopeless—were rough but inspiring. My brother Roger and I knew we were dirt poor; having to wear shoes made from hollowed-out cow dung was a dead giveaway. Even so, we didn't mind, because in Arkansas in those days there was nothing to do even if you were rich. Remember, a seven-year-old boy couldn't go to a house of prostitution. You had to wait until you were ten to do that.

That's why it was a very big day in Hopeless when word got around that a new restaurant was opening up in Little Rock—the finest restaurant Arkansas had ever seen. It served hamburgers, cheeseburgers, and even French fries. Imagine that, potatoes flown in to humble Arkansas all the way from Paris! That restaurant has since blossomed into an international success story and a symbol of American quality and good taste. That restaurant, of course, was McDonald's.

Here's a little secret about your President that only my closest friends know: I still enjoy visiting McDonald's every now and then, ordering up three or four of their Happy Meals and savoring the delicious food while I assemble the Flintstones cars. And each time I get my order and my Secret Service men reach for their wallets, it always amazes me how McDonald's manages to keep its prices so low.

In those days, of course, the prices were even lower. McDonald's had a slogan then that went something like this: "A hamburger, soda and fries, and change back from your dollar." And when my brother Roger and I would visit that McDonald's to beg for food, I saw with my own eyes people's reaction to getting that change: They invariably thanked the counterperson and walked away with a smile. "They want it," I thought to myself. "People want their change." And just as I have never quite lost my taste for McDonald's fries, I have never quite lost my belief that people want change.

My friends, when you elected me President of this great nation with forty-three percent of the vote, you proved me right. In a thundering voice you cried out your mandate: "Almost half the people in America want change!" I have attempted to provide you with that

change. I have not always been successful. I have not often been successful. But just as a Big Mac reheated any time within a year of purchase retains its essential flavor and nutritional benefits, so my promise of quick, dramatic governmental change remains firm and unwavering, despite the fact that it now looks as though it will have to be incremental and wait until my second term.

That's where you come in. My job is to understand my mistakes and recover from them. Your job is to reelect me if you believe I've done so. It's that simple.

What's my job?

Why, you're the First Lady, of course. One of the loveliest and most gracious First Ladies the Nation has ever seen.

I mean what's my job in the next Administration? This health care thing is getting old. I want a Cabinet post.

You're so funny, Hillary!

I mean it. Dump Christopher. I can handle State.

We can discuss this later, dear. Not in front of the V-O-T-E-R-S.

Fine. But you owe me, Casanova. Remember that.

RECOVERING FROM ATTACKS BY THE OPPOSITION PARTY

If you're going to make a career of public service, as I have, you must expect to endure some experiences that are going to be less than edifying. No one likes to have their political philosophy questioned. Or their style of governing. Or their authority. Or their veracity. Or their character. Or their sincerity. Or their humility. Or their accountability. Or their reliability. Or their integrity. Or their ability. Or their honesty. Or their will. Or their morality. Or their strength. Or their intelligence. Or their decency. Or their empathy. Or their fidelity. Or their probity . . . What was I talking about again?

RECOVERING FROM ATTACKS BY THE PRESS

Hey. You know they're a pack of dogs. I know they're a pack of dogs. But my fate is in the hands of my Higher Power, not some hairspray-wearing jackal with a lavaliere mike on his lapel and a million-dollar paycheck in his wallet. And when Peter "Canadian? *Me?* Don't be silly!" Jennings comes at me with aggressive questions, the Lord has instructed me to smile and deny, smile and deny, smile and deny, and then call Immigration and check on his work visa.

RECOVERING FROM ATTACKS BY THE WIFE

You know what's embarrassing? You're standing in the White House Rose Garden for a photo opportunity with King Hussein. They've just had one of those twenty-four hour periods in the Middle East where nobody killed each other, and he's staying at your place for a few days while the two of you take credit, and in between pictures he turns to you with a chuckle and says, "What was all that shrieking last night? You slaughter your own poultry here?" Remember, he comes from a region where they force their women to wear black shrouds, and here you've got to say to him, "Oh, that was the wife. We were having a little disagreement."

Nobody needs a day like that, particularly if you've got a crackerjack security force at your disposal. If you sense an impending attack by your spouse, hit the buzzer. When Secret Service arrives, explain the problem, authorize the tranquilizer, make sure she's tucked in and comfortable, and then shake off those bad feelings by doing something for yourself. Maybe a spur-of-the-moment helicopter trip to Atlantic City, completely unplanned. Have someone go out a week or so in advance to scout the waitresses.

Chapter Two

FALSE PATHS TO SOLACE

You've heard it said before. It's lonely being the President. The burdens of the office force you to lose touch with the "real" people who elected you, and the people you *do* see every day, your staff, are afraid to disagree with you or even divulge any news you might find unwelcome. In an administration like mine, if your subordinates are afraid to bring you bad news, you can go months without talking to a soul.

It's pretty lonely in other ways too. I mean, let's say hypothetically that you're the governor of a small state. It's not out of the question that you might go to a governors' convention or a New Democrats weekend retreat and meet some hot young legislative aide receptive to the idea of strategically channeling seed money into a relief program. But when you're President, the only conferences you get to go to are with heads of state, and who are you supposed to nail at one of those? Margaret Thatcher? Indira Gandhi? Believe me, it's no coincidence that I never ran for high office until after those two bow-wows were out of the picture.

So loneliness is an occupational hazard for any President. For a *dysfunctional* President who hasn't yet discovered the Twelve Steps, loneliness can be downright dangerous. Without a trusted friend or loved one to steer us toward a positive path of recovery, we are apt to try to find solace in "quick fix" solutions that are invariably shallow and ineffective, no matter how much they make us go off like an H-bomb at the time.

The problem is that substitute pleasures can quickly become as addictive as what they have replaced. Let's say you are trying to ease the pain of another rejection by Congress, and you decide to forget it momentarily through the simple and relatively benign act of jogging over to the nearest Taco Bell and ordering a Seven Layer Burrito. How much harm can there be in that? But as soon as you polish that burrito off, those sad feelings come back, and you start seeing Gingrich's fat face in the dregs of your refried beans, and before you know it you're ordering another burrito. And if your experience with Congress is anything like mine, very soon you're wolfing down twenty or thirty burritos at a sitting and having to grin and bear it when Peter Jennings makes remarks like, "That was a very forceful State of the Union Address by our chubby Chief Executive." And it's the same with any other addiction substitute, be it saxophone playing, cigar smoking, $200 haircuts, or that old standby, s-e-x. Speaking hypothetically, there aren't enough Stuckey's waitresses in the world to see a President through two terms of trying to pass health care legislation. There has to be something else.

And that something else, of course, is the Twelve Steps. Only when we look ourselves in the mirror, square our shoulders, face our demons and proclaim loudly and firmly, "None of this is my fault," can we begin to really address what is wrong.

How do we know when that time has come? That's what the next chapter is all about.

I would just like to add here that if isolation is a chronic problem for male world leaders who look around an international conference and see only Thatchers and Gandhis, perhaps the American public should consider electing a *woman* President. It may well be true that there aren't enough Stuckey's waitresses to last through eight years of trying to pass a health bill, but I'll bet there are more than enough horny insurance industry lobbyists to do it.

In any case, looking at the problem of false solutions from a woman's viewpoint, I would add that those activities that are traditionally considered part of a "woman's" role—cooking, cleaning, the raising of children—are not effective substitutes for recovery either. When I made a remark during the 1992 campaign about not staying home and baking cookies, it was widely regarded as contemptuous of more traditional women. Nothing could be further from the truth. My meaning, twisted as usual by the press, was that baking cookies does not really help anyone work through their problems, and that I was incensed at the oppressive males who had convinced generations of women that it would.

Contempt for traditional women? On the contrary, I feel great *empathy for* and *solidarity with* those unimaginative losers who can't conceive of any life beyond the benighted quasi-existence of their tyrannized mothers. That's why I'd rather slit my wrists than live the way they do. Or, to look at it from another perspective, I know that I couldn't possibly make the commitment of time and energy and the emotional investment necessary to raise children the way I believe they should be raised. And since I can't do it perfectly, I choose not to do it at all. That's the reason I never had children.

But we have a child, dear. Our daughter, Chelsea.

Oh yes, you're right! And she's a constant source of joy to us both.

She certainly is.

Chelsea, right?

RECOVERING FROM INFIDELITY

"The spirit is willing, but the flesh is weak." Ah, don't I know it! Uh, in the abstract, I mean. Infidelity is a very common frailty, a trait of our species and as such not something we can be "blamed" for, but nevertheless it's always accompanied by a piercing, unique sort of guilt. Or so I'm told. In any case, time is a great healer. If you *have* strayed, try not to beat up on yourself. Acknowledge that you are human, and as a human, you are flawed and not in control of your own fate. Put the matter in the hands of God. Give yourself a break. You have faltered today, but tomorrow you will be better.

RECOVERING FROM YOUR SPOUSE'S LEARNING OF YOUR INFIDELITY

When you have been unfaithful, your spouse is bound to feel betrayed. There may be anger and resentment on her part, however misguided, and therefore it is usually best to break the news to her in a room free of sharp-edged Arkansas Razorback knick-knacks. Apologize to your spouse. Explain that you never meant to hurt her. Tell her the unfortunate incident is now in the past. If your marriage is built on a solid foundation of love, she will understand—and your relationship will be the better for it.

RECOVERING FROM YOUR SPOUSE'S INFIDELITY

Some things just can't be tolerated. Send her packing.

Chapter Three

THE MOMENT OF
REALIZATION

How and why do we know when it's time for us to seek help? There is no single answer, no "magic" indicator that our term as President has reached critical mass. One President might wake up the morning after his party loses Congress in a humiliating election rout and think, "Hmm, I wonder if the voters are entirely happy with the job we've been doing."

Another President might be served with papers from some shyster lawyer representing a bimbo. Upon examining those papers he might learn that they require him to show his winkie to a grand jury, in order to investigate the woman's claim that she can identify a series of freckles on it in the shape of Orion the Hunter. "How do I explain to Yeltsin that my love pump is the lead story on *Hard Copy?*" he might ask himself. "Perhaps I need help."

Still another President might find that, while enjoying some classic silent films in the White House screening room, he is suddenly standing on a chair, shaking his fist at the screen on which Lon Chaney is playing the Phantom of the Opera, and screaming, "You'll never get me, Dole! You'll never get me!" And once again, he may interpret this as a possible clue that something is wrong.

For me, though, the moment of truth was not a cataclysmic event in any way. In fact, it happened while I was shaving.

I was looking in the mirror, practicing a speech for the Joint Chiefs of Staff. "It is absolutely vital that we continue to discourage, by military force if need be, the denial of human rights anywhere on this planet . . . Unless, of course, that would get us into trouble or make people not like us, in which case I guess the best thing to do is send that spineless old woman Jimmy Carter over there to ignore official policy and give away the store to Gadhafi—"

And that's when I saw the light.

Well, not the light exactly. What I actually saw, while shaving that tricky area just under my nose, was some sort of a bump at the corner of my lip. "OH MY GOD!" I said. "IT'S A CHANCRE! I'VE GONE AND DONE IT! I GOT MYSELF HERPED UP! NOBODY'S GONNA WANT TO VOTE FOR A PRESIDENT WITH A BIG-ASS HERPES SORE ON HIS FACE! WAIT 'TIL *THE NEW YORK TIMES* SEES THIS! OH LORDY LORDY, HILLARY IS GONNA HAVE MY OYSTERS NAILED TO A PLANK AND HOISTED TO THE TOP OF THE WHITE HOUSE FLAGPOLE! WHY COULDN'T I HAVE KEPT LITTLE ELVIS IN MY PANTS—WAIT! WAIT! WHAT IF IT'S *NOT A CHANCRE*? WHAT IF IT'S SOMETHING WORSE?" In my panic, I couldn't help but touch the little lump of diseased flesh. It fell off my face into the soapy water of the sink.

I fished it out, and what I had thought was a chancre turned out to be nothing more malignant than the undercooked tip of a McDonald's French fry. I did not have a disease. I had been spared. And yet I was so shaken by the experience that I barely tasted that French fry morsel as it went down.

My fellow Americans, that was the moment I realized I needed help. My presidency had become such a fragile entity that it was threatened by a tiny fragment of potato. Not even Nixon was afraid of tubers. It was time to get control of my life, get control of my presidency, get control of Little Elvis and turn things around.

My own moment of realization came one November morning, after Bill had been re-elected Governor of Arkansas for the third or fourth time. I'd lost track. Anyway, I should have been celebrating, but all I could think about was chickens. Chickens. Roasted, boiled, fried, barbecued, jerked chickens. See, the Arkansas poultry industry had always supported Bill, appreciating his vision, his commitment, his being too busy raising taxes to notice that processed chicken and processed chicken fecal matter often look quite similar. Every time Bill won an election, they'd send over a truckload of congratulatory chickens for our use.

It's just amazing how many chickens they can fit into one of those trucks. Did you know that wedged in good and tight, your average chicken takes up no more room than a softball with a beak? You can stack 'em up ten or twenty layers deep, and after a while most of 'em don't make a peep. They'd always bury a little campaign contribution somewhere in the truck among the chickens, and we'd let Chelsea dive in there and look for it. You know, like an Easter egg hunt.

There I stood, knowing that truck was on the way . . . when something clicked in my mind. I knew at that moment that I couldn't take any more chickens. I wanted to be elected—er, *Bill* to be elected to an office where the gifts would be coming from *all* levels of the food pyramid. I wanted gene-altering cattle ranchers to be sending us Texas steaks, I wanted irradiating vegetable farmers to be shipping us New Jersey tomatoes, I wanted pesticide-spraying fruit wholesalers to be mailing us Georgia peaches. I wanted my husband to be President.

That's a wonderful story, Hillary. But how does it tie in to recovery?

Like this: I want to give the American people my solemn word that I will do whatever is necessary to make sure you recover in time for a triumphant second term, no matter how hard the road ahead, no matter how difficult the trials you face—even if it kills you. Because I'm not going back to Chicken Shit, USA, you hear me, farm boy?

I love you, sweetheart.

And I love *you*.

RECOVERING FROM THE SPEAKER OF THE HOUSE'S MOTHER WHISPERING TO CONNIE CHUNG THAT HER SON CALLED YOUR WIFE THE B-WORD

Politics is a funny thing. You can't behave in the White House the way you would in a bar, or on a duck-hunting trip. I'm not just talking about personal hygiene here. Let's say you're down at the local tavern, and some guy calls your wife a name. Even if you think he sort of has a point, you have to stand up for her, no question about it, and maybe pop the fat little jerk in the mouth. But as the President, you can't do that. You have to show a little grace. So you get your wife to invite the guy and his mother to the White House, you know, show the press how you can turn the other cheek, and the four of you end up doing Wild Turkey shots (well, Hillary's was cream soda) and having a pretty good time, and the funny thing is you really do forgive the guy for what he said. Although I suppose part of that is sheer relief and gratitude to your Higher Power that Connie Chung wasn't at breakfast last week to hear what *you* called your wife. Anyway, it's no big deal, really. Let's face it—if I had a dime for every time "bitch" was used in the same sentence as Hillary's name, I could eliminate the deficit overnight.

Hey! An insult tax! Get me the I.R.S.!

RECOVERING FROM BEING STALKED
BY A LUNATIC

There are few things in life more chilling than realizing you are being stalked—because there are few types of human beings more frightening than the obsessive stalker. He is a man driven by need: a desperate, frenetic need to be recognized, to be acknowledged, to feel, even if only for one brief moment, the glare of the world's attention. He is a sick, sick creature. Fortunately, if you just wait until you hear his footsteps get close enough and then whirl around, shake him by the shoulders and in a loud, firm voice exclaim, "Go home, Perot!" that usually does the trick.

Chapter Four

HOME-BREWED RECOVERY:

YOU CAN'T DO IT ALL YOURSELF. HELL, YOU CAN'T DO ANY OF IT YOURSELF

The moment at which we realize we need a Greater Power's help is both glorious and terrifying, kind of like the moment when, after you've been sitting for three or four hours nursing the same cup of coffee and bottomless plate of Stuckey's onion rings, the waitress finally agrees to take a peek at Orion the Hunter—and only then do you realize that you don't know her name.

At least that's my impression, based on hearing that rascally bachelor Stephanopoulos tell it. What I'm trying to say is, to understand that things have gotten out of your control—that's liberating. But to also understand that to change, you'll need the help of a Higher Power— that's truly frightening. Particularly for those of us who, over the course of the years, may have made one or two campaign promises in our prayers that we perhaps have not technically delivered on. (It's very easy to say, "Oh dear Jesus, you hand over Boone County on the third of November and I swear to you I will never stray from the sanctity of the marital bed again." It's another thing to realize six months later that, yes, you've once again held onto the governorship by your cuticles. But your state's still an outtake from "Deliverance," your wife's still a leading contender for the local Toughman belt, the biggest thing you have to look forward to this year is passing a law requiring your teachers to be able to write their own names, and the only thing stopping you from jumping out the Statehouse window—besides the fact that the Statehouse is only two stories high—is that you don't want to die without having found out whether the waitress is really and truly a blonde. There's no point in being coy about it; we've all had those feelings.)

What was I saying? Oh, yeah. So even though we know we need help, we may not yet be ready to receive that help from our Higher Power. A natural and very common wish is that somehow, some way, we may be able to treat ourselves.

It's an attractive idea, certainly. But can a stopped clock be expected to wind and reset itself? No. Can a car change its own flat tire? Of course not. Can a leper, seeing the last of his ten fingers fall off his hand onto the ground, be expected to pick it up and reattach it by himself? No. Someone must pick that finger up and give it to him. As a recovering President, I am like that leper—but with a difference. Not just anyone can come to my aid and return that finger. God has to give me the finger. And I believe he has.

In other words, we won't find the source of our recovery here on earth. Racked by guilt, we may become convinced that just confessing our transgressions will somehow be enough. But confess to whom? The person or persons we have wronged? My friends, if you've ever been chased around the Governor's Mansion at four in the morning by a crazed attorney wielding sheep shears and shrieking that she'll have your oysters for breakfast, you know that's not a good idea.

Who, then? A member of the clergy? A fellow head of state? Not too many months ago, troubled by the course of world events, I had the opportunity to unburden myself to a wonderful man who is both an ordained priest *and* the president of one of our Caribbean neighbor nations. Because of some political misunderstandings in his own land of Haiti, President Aristede was at that time living in the White House basement, on a futon we'd set up in the bowling alley. I dropped down to see him one night when I was having trouble sleeping and the idiots in the kitchen had forgotten to order me a pizza.

"Jean Bertrand," I said. "The Congress seems determined to humiliate me. The voters are turning against me. There's this chick who says she can identify a constellation on my wanger. And I just can't get away from the feeling that, somehow, at least some of this is my own fault. What can I do, Jean Bertrand, what can I do?"

Thoughtfully he replied, "You indecisive, incompetent loser, when are you gonna invade my country and get me my job back, you wuss?" Well, you know how I hate to disappoint anyone. Before I knew it, my urge to confess had led to confrontation with Haiti's leaders, an invasion ordered and averted and, ultimately, more glory for that popeyed old nellie Jimmy Carter while I get branded "wishy-washy." Fellow Americans, I am at heart a peaceful man, and I never get the urge to sneak up behind any of the other ex-presidents and yank their underwear. It's just not what I'm about. But Jimmy Carter better not ever turn his back on me, unless he wants an atomic wedgie that Rosalynn will still be trying to loosen when the old queen finally steps up to receive his Nobel Peace Prize—sometime around the year Three Zillion A.D., if I have anything to say about it.

I keep getting sidetracked. I was trying to say that no matter whom you confide in—your spouse, another president, a flight attendant smuggled into Camp David for your birthday—you can almost bet that the results will be less than satisfactory, because none of these beings is a Higher Power, except maybe the flight attendant. What can you do, then, to release yourself from your shortcomings? Self-inflicted pain? It may have worked in the Bible, but you try jogging down Pennsylvania Avenue wearing a hair shirt in August and see if it perks *you* up. Self-flagellation? Again, hopelessly archaic, although you might get some kind of whip thing going with the flight attendant later when you're feeling better. Atoning by doing good works? Hell, even *finding* a good work you can do while Auntie Jimmy Carter's hovering around is like trying to find the Chivas in the liquor cabinet when my brother Roger's visiting.

No. I wish there were some way a President in need could heal himself, but there is not. There is only one way—the Twelve-Step way. And having attained that realization, we will shortly examine those Steps, one by one.

Incidentally, for reasons of national security I'm not showing this chapter to Hillary, so don't mention it to her, okay?

Bill, where's that chapter you were putting together on trying to recover without outside help? I'm ready to write my portion of it.

Oh, hi honey. Uh, I decided not to do that chapter.

I see. By the way, what's this notepaper I found from the TWA Flight Attendants Training Academy? It seems to have some of your writing on it.

Hmm? Yeah, um, Stephanopoulos left that here. I guess I scribbled some ideas on it. You can throw that out. That George is a wild one!

Yeah. That George is a wild one. You think he needs this phone number you wrote on here?

Uh, no, I'm sure he doesn't need that.

Good.

RECOVERING FROM UNTRUE STATEMENTS ABOUT YOUR PAST

There's an old saying about how the lie gets printed on page one and the retraction on page twenty, and I'm afraid that maxim doesn't apply only to the federal budget. Though the Twelve Steps instruct us to try to get on the good side of everyone but Gingrich and Dole, there will always be people with their own agenda who cannot be dissuaded from spreading falsehood and innuendo concerning your interaction with a hefty chunk of Arkansas's female population. But just as I have put my fate in the hands of my Higher Power, I must trust my Higher Power to show the American public that the people circulating these stories are liars, liars, liars. It's also a pretty good idea to slap an IRS audit on each of them. Not out of vindictiveness, mind you, but just to keep them busy. Idle hands and all that.

RECOVERING FROM TRUE STATEMENTS
ABOUT YOUR PAST

This one's a little trickier, because, of course, what's done can't be undone. But, hey, everyone makes mistakes, you know? Who among us hasn't written his draft board a long letter explaining why he reneged on his promise to enter ROTC once the danger of being drafted had passed, or spent hours and hours in taped phone conversations with a bimbo he claimed to know only casually, or signed all sorts of documents linking him to a real estate deal that violated every regulation in the book? My Higher Power is making me a good person today and a better person tomorrow. As Fleetwood Mac says, "Yesterday's gone." I just wish yesterday's goddamn paperwork were gone, too.

Chapter Five

MAKING THE BIG LEAP
INTO RECOVERY

All right. Now we know why we need to recover, and we know what we must do to recover. So why are we still standing on recovery's shore, gingerly testing the water with our big toe, instead of splashing and laughing and soaping up our firm young thighs in the water with all the other Miss Arkansas contestants?

I may have gotten my metaphors a little mixed there, but you know what I mean. What holds us back, of course, is fear. Fear that we lack the strength to recover. Well, my fellow Americans, there is strength in numbers. That's why an essential component of my Twelve-Step program is healthy group discussion—talking it through with respect, support and love.

Just listen to this excerpt from a recent White House recovery session. Of course I have changed the names of all participants in order to protect their privacy. Even Lloyd Bentsen's, the quitter. We join the session already in progress:

"Sal": Mister President, I move that we bring this session to a close. I mean, we've been at it for three hours now, and as far as I can tell you're the only one in the group who thinks we have a problem.

"Jeffanopoulos": Oh, you've obviously got a problem, Gore. Your problem is a ten-foot stick up your ass. Why don't you stop pacing around like your spine is fused and give the President a chance?

"Sal": It's "Mister Vice President" to you, four-eyes! And at least I've *got* a spine!

"Jeffanopoulos": Too bad you haven't got a clue!

"Sal": Get a haircut!

"Jeffanopoulos": Take an enema!

"Sandra": I *like* his hair!

"Will": Al! George! Barbra! Stop it! The fact is, when this Administration fails to serve the people, we've *all* got a problem.

"Todd": I agree. And the problem is not eased at all by this sort of petty infighting.

"Sal": Ooh, the Elder Statesman has spoken.

"Jeffanopoulos": Really. Tell us again what things were like under Truman, pops.

"Todd": Hey, little boy, I knew Harry Truman. I served with Harry Truman. Let me tell you something—

"Jeffanopoulos": Spare me, grandpa.

"Todd": That's it. I quit. I'm going back to my ranch.

"Jeffanopoulos": God's waiting room.

"Todd": I heard that!

"Harriet": STOP IT! STOP IT! Bill's mind is made up! He has a plan! Let him speak!

"Will": That's right, my mind is made up. Although, now that I think about it, maybe we need to examine the situation a little more—

"Harriet": TELL THEM THE PLAN, YOU JELLY-FISH!

"Will": Okay. Here's the plan Hillary came up with. *"Harriet"*: Hillary and *I*.

"Will": The plan Hillary and I came up with. Number one. I go on the three major networks and admit the Administration has a problem.

[Sounds indicating general assent]

"Sandra": Maybe you can open with a couple of jokes or something to warm people up. Maybe a song?

"Sal": That doesn't sound very presidential.

"Sandra": So sue me.

"Jeffanopoulos": You're not even supposed to be here, Streisand.

"Sandra": I'm welcome anywhere I choose to go! My music is adored all over the planet!

"Jeffanopoulos": Yeah? Then either sing "On A Clear Day" or shut up and leave the politics to the pros!

"Harriet": I think maybe you should go a little easier on the double espressos, George.

"Jeffanopoulos": Yes, Mrs. Clinton.

"Will": Number two. I outline the actions we are planning to take to resolve that problem, including the implementation of my Twelve-Step plan for all White House and Cabinet personnel.

[Sounds indicating general assent]

"Will": Number three. While I am busy recovering under the plan, I sign an executive order temporarily turning the office of the President over to my wife, who—Wait a minute, I don't remember this!

"Harriet": Oh, I put that in after you went to bed. I didn't want to disturb you.

"Will": Now hold on a minute, honey . . .

Well, maybe this didn't turn out to be the best example of a recovery session I could have chosen. But you get the idea. Within the safety and security of a sympathetic group, we find the strength to take strides that we might not otherwise.

I still think that temporary-president idea was good. It would have let you concentrate on getting well.

You know, I actually feel a lot better already.

RECOVERING FROM THE JOINT CHIEFS REFUSING TO COME TO THE WHITE HOUSE FOR A SCREENING OF *LA CAGE AUX FOLLES*

I thought it would help them work through this Gays in the Military thing, okay? Man, you can't blame a guy for trying. Ten bowls of Cheetos and I had to eat them all myself. I could hardly get through dinner.

RECOVERING FROM MISSTATEMENTS

Everyone says something stupid now and then, but not everyone gets on the front page of the *New York Times* when they do it. I do suffer occasional lapses of judgement. Who doesn't? Sometimes I can be a little insensitive to people's feelings, like the time I invited Mario Cuomo to a strategy dinner and asked him if he felt like eating wop. Sometimes my own eagerness to learn leads to a question at an inappropriate moment, like when I asked John F. Kennedy Jr. at his mother's funeral whether Daryl Hannah bucks like a bronco. My fellow Americans, I'm only human. I make mistakes *on occasion*. But I can guarantee you this: I know how to spell potato.

Speaking of which, I'm starting to feel a little hungry. Wonder if we've got any of those Cheetos left?

Chapter Six

THE TWELUE STEPS:

THE TRUE ANSWER

Now we have again reached the essential part of my Twelve-Step program: the Twelve Steps themselves. Let's review all of them together, and then analyze them one by one.

The Twelve Steps to Political Recovery

1. We admit that we have become powerless over Congress and we cannot accomplish anything in the first term.

2. We realize that if we are to achieve a second term, we will need help from a Greater Power. Quite a bit of help, actually.

3. We make a decision to turn our will and our lives over to that Power, which we have learned through governing a state in the Bible Belt to call God.

4. We take stock of ourselves unsparingly and take note of our flaws, no matter how tremendously overshadowed they are by our stellar qualities.

5. We tell God everything that's wrong with ourselves, and ask Him how much of it is likely to come out during the campaign.

6. We tell God we're ready to have Him remove all defects of character, and humbly ask His permission to leak the good news.

7. We respectfully ask Him to get it done before the New Hampshire primary.

8. We make a list of political enemies we've made and determine their influence in Congress, the media and the public arena.

9. We kiss up to as many of those people as possible and promise appointments to the rest.

10. We keep making lists of everything wrong with us, on the slim chance that we'll be ready the next time the media unearths something we did in the '80s.

11. We keep trying to get on God's good side. And everyone else's too, except those pricks Gingrich and Dole, who don't have one.

12. We carry our message of redemption and reelection to others through sound bites, photo ops and the occasional interminable speech.

It seems like such a simple program, doesn't it? And that is precisely its beauty and its strength. One of the most important things I have learned as your President is that people like proposals that are clearly stated and easy to follow. Especially those hydrocephalic snakes in Congress, who are deathly afraid that if they vote for a bill that is the least bit complex they might at some point be called upon to actually explain it to their constituents. Okay, I'm willing to admit when I've made a mistake. Maybe a ten-thousand page health bill was too long even for those senators and representatives who don't move their lips when they read. Maybe you think that if the bill had been half that length, or a quarter that length, it might have had a virgin's chance in Little Rock of passing. Well, I see your point, you're absolutely right, and next time I will do better. (Perhaps you suspect the fault is not completely mine, that the blame for all those pages and pages of legalistic mumbo jumbo should rest entirely with a certain Little Miss Yale Law School, but I won't shirk my responsibility for what happened.

Besides, Hillary and I have pledged to support each other in our legislative efforts, no matter how needlessly obtuse or show-offy they may be.)

You think the health bill was too complex? Why don't you show them the original draft of your Twelve-Step program, the one with 250 steps?

Now, sweetheart, I just put that in because of what the polls said about us always trying to pass overly complicated programs. You know as soon as I'm reelected the first thing we're going to do is ram that bill down Dole's throat with a broomstick—I mean, work together with Congress to pass meaningful health-care legislation.

Just remember, farm boy, that when I met you, you couldn't *count* to twelve.

And you couldn't count to twenty-eight, could you? Or we wouldn't be married today. Now where was I? Damn it, I hate to keep getting sidetracked like this. It reminds me too much of Cabinet meetings.

Oh yeah, I was saying that the beauty of the Twelve-Step program is that it's *simple* and *easy to understand. Simple* and *Easy,* you hear that, Mrs. Oliver Wendell Holmes?

I guess she's gone. Probably went to some hen party at NOW. Don't worry, she'll be back when she cools off a little. This is nothing. You should have seen her when I suggested we give the Medal of Freedom to Sharon Stone.

So, like I said, simple and easy to understand. Let's go through the Steps one by one and I'll show you what I mean.

RECOVERING FROM ONE TOO MANY BIG GULPS

It is easy for a President to lose touch with the people, and that is something I have sworn never to let happen. So I go where the people go, do what the people do, eat what the people eat, and drink what the people drink. The people are drinking Big Gulps; I, as their leader, must also drink Big Gulps. I mean, those suckers are good! The problem, of course, is that after drinking their Big Gulps the people don't have to sit in a wooden chair in an international economic summit for eight hours straight with C-SPAN's cameras recording every fidget. I trust in my Higher Power, of course, but it helps to have a catheter, a coffee can and Stephanopoulos under the conference table hooking everything up.

RECOVERING FROM PROMISING A SITCOM PRODUCER THAT HE COULD BE SECRETARY OF STATE

Look, Harry Thomason's a good guy—that *Evening Shade* was a crackup! I really had the best intentions. I mean, a producer and a secretary of state have to utilize many of the same abilities. Uh, knowing how to negotiate. Er, good listening skills. Um, willingness to travel. Uh, um . . . Christ, I will never, never, *never* drink Sambuca again.

Step One. We Admit that We Have Become Powerless Over Congress and We Cannot Accomplish Anything in the First Term.

Well, that one seems pretty self-explanatory, right? But there's a catch. It's easy to admit you're powerless; what's important is that you make that admission *without any negative feelings attached*. Bitterness and rancor are counterproductive. After all, the people elect a man President, a young, dynamic—dare I say handsome?—man, a man with a vision for the nation's future, because they're tired of twelve years of Republican stagnation where the "grand plan" is to keep the rich white people in power by doing absolutely nothing. And when this young man gets to Washington, full of hope and promise and raring to shake things up, the obstructionist Congress nails him to a cross of "No" votes and leaves him hanging there in the wind while well-financed right-wing character assassins feed the press a steady stream of rumors. Soon the media jackals are foaming at the mouth, all trying to bite off the biggest piece of the President, and meanwhile the voters once again reveal the limitless depths of their stupidity by turning Congress over to the same troglodytes who have kept it paralyzed for two years. And with all these powerful forces massed and pounding against him like waves and waves of human shit, it's no wonder the embattled President can't attain a single one of his noble goals and must admit, in Step One, that the vile, inhuman scum have won. But as I wrote earlier, there's no point in griping about it. As your President you won't hear me do so.

Well done, dear. Reasoned, forceful, compelling.

I don't know. I'm a little concerned with what I said about Congress and the press.

It *was* a bit mild, but you're the President. You have to be diplomatic.

RECOVERING FROM FINANCIAL SCANDAL

I don't get it. The First Lady unveils a health care plan that will cost a few billion dollars to implement, and she gets all this criticism for being bad with money. Then it comes out that she parlayed a thousand dollars in stock options into a hundred thousand, and she gets crap from the critics for being too *good* with money. Which is it going to be, people? I admit it looks bad for the wife of a public servant to make more money playing the market than a trainload of Arkansas schoolteachers earns in a decade, but there was nothing improper or unethical about what she did. She got lucky, that's all. You know what she does? She's got a dart board—actually a bunch of them, one marked "Commodities Futures," one marked "Index Options," one marked "Emerging Issues"— and she puts on this little blindfold left over from a Pin the Tail on the Donkey game at one of Chelsea's birthday parties, and then she turns around and holds her breath and tosses the darts over her shoulder at the boards. It's cute, really. Harmless. Totally innocent. Then she calls up Alan Greenspan over at the Fed and tells him to goose her portfolio or else.

Step Two. We Realize That If We Are to Achieve a Second Term, We Will Need Help from a Greater Power. Quite a Bit of Help, Actually.

This Step is where we begin to recapture our humility. As I mentioned earlier, the Oval Office is the loneliest place in Washington. You have no peer group to monitor your performance. If I were a senator, I could hang around with other senators and figure out how I was doing. If I were a Supreme Court justice, I could hang around with other justices. But I'm a member of a tiny club—I'm President. Not only that, I'm a Democratic President from the South. How many of *those* are there to hang around with? Don't even say it.

So as a natural outgrowth of all that loneliness, you begin to think that the only human being you can rely on is yourself. This feeling is doubly reinforced when half your personnel is barely into puberty and your Chief of Staff is a former Ford dealer whose response every time some hack senator mounts a filibuster is to run up and down the White House corridors in a panic attack, shouting, "We gotta move some of these Torinos!"

But the truth is, you *cant* rely on yourself. Not to do it all. I don't care what subtle clue finally convinces you—the all-time-record low popularity polls, the failure of all your legislative initiatives, the cost of an attorney to keep the Grand Jury from getting a look at your noodle— sooner or later the little refrigerator light in your head will go off and you will understand that your fate is not in your own hands.

I've been telling you that for years.

No, sweetheart, I didn't mean that it's in *your* hands.

Whose else could it be in?

I'm getting into the realm of the spiritual here.

Oh. Well then, wake me when it's over.

RECOVERING FROM HAVING AN EMBARRASING YOUNGER SIBLING

I'm going to reveal something I've never told anyone before: I'm not easily embarrassed. I mean, once or twice in my career I've been caught telling a little fib—these were all before my recovery, of course— but usually I could get out of it by just twisting my finger into my cheek, batting my eyes and saying, "Biwwy was a bad Pwesident again. Biwwy sowwy." My brother Roger, though—Jesus! What a doof! What am I supposed to do? I've tried telling myself that he's good for the balance of trade and the U.S.'s relationship with Colombia. At one staff meeting, I even floated the idea of naming him Vice President, to ensure that no one would take a shot at me. If you'd ever heard Al Gore sob you'd know why I dropped that idea in a hurry.

For weeks I wrestled with the problem. Then, at dinner with Sharon Stone one night—hey, lighten up, it was an official state dinner, there were lots of other people there, that guy, what's his name, that Mandela guy was there too—it came to me. The good people of the entertainment community have always been an important cornerstone of my constituency, and they are people who I believe can appreciate Roger's skills and experience. Therefore, as soon as I'm reelected, I will name Roger the President's Special Liaison for Hollywood Party Supplies. See? My Higher Power found a way. I just hope Roger doesn't blow it. "Blow" it. Get the joke?

Step Three. We Make a Decision to Turn Our Will and Our Lives Over to that Power, Which We Have Learned Through Governing a State in the Bible Belt to Call God.

This Step is really the crux of the entire program—and the most difficult Step to take. Make a decision? Do I have to? There's something so absolute and final about sticking to one choice. When the menu offers a Big Mac, a Quarter Pounder and a McLean Deluxe, why should you only be able to polish off one of them? When you've got a Veteran's Hall full of lovely and easily impressed young women vying for the title of Miss Arkansas, why should you only be able to polish off one of *them*? Why *can't* I have two Korea policies, three Haiti policies, and four Bosnia policies?

Because Stephanopoulos says it makes me look piggy, that's why. And I'm not a piggy. I'm the President. So when it's time for me to make a decision, I've got to rub my hands together, hitch up my pants, and do it.

On the other hand, maybe it's best not to rush into anything.

No. No. I'm going to do it. I'm doing it. I've done it! I've turned my will over to my Higher Power—and it feels great! Because no matter what happens now, it's not my fault! I didn't fire everyone in the White House travel office and replace them with my third cousin. God did it. I didn't bring air traffic at Los Angeles International to a standstill while I sat inside Air Force One getting my nose hairs trimmed. God did it. *I* didn't tell Janet Reno to go ahead and lean on that David Koresh guy a little bit. God did it. Man, I wish I'd thought of this years ago. I've got Divine Deniability.

Yes, I've done it. I've placed my will and my life into God's hands. And that leaves you the voters with a pretty clear path, in my opinion. But if the thought of being visited by locusts and boils and such interests you, fine, go ahead and vote for someone else in '96. Maybe you've got enough canned goods in the basement to last you until God cools off.

As for why I call my Higher Power *God*, I'll have more to say about that in the next chapter. For now, just remember that—unlike the intolerant religious fanatics now dominating a certain political party—I believe all Americans have the right to worship or not according to their own beliefs. Even though I myself am forced to go to church every goddamn week or risk Gingrich accusing me of devil worship.

What about those innocent five-year-olds who would be tarred and feathered by their fundamentalist classmates for not participating in the "voluntary" school prayer you support? What about their rights?

They're much too young to vote. Besides, I can always go on Nickelodeon or something and tell them it was a big mistake. Or grant an interview to one of those Power Rangers. Maybe the pink one. What's her name?

Let me just review here for a minute. You've put your will and life into God's hands, and He's dictating policy. Therefore a vote against you is a vote against God.

Right.

Okay. But what if the voters also put their lives and wills into God's hands, and then they go to the polls in November '96 and you *still* lose every state, the District of Columbia, Puerto Rico and Guam? Who is doing God's will then?

What a ridiculous question. I am.

How do you know?

I can feel it.

Bill, have you been talking to Streisand again?

Look. If they voted me out, that would simply mean they *thought* they'd put themselves in God's hands, but in reality they were still trying to make their own decisions. It's a problem common to Twelve Steppers everywhere, and all it means is that you haven't made as much progress as you think you have, and you need to back up a little and try again.

Bill, you idiot, there won't be any "backing up and trying again." If they vote you out, they vote you out! This isn't Arkansas, where you can lose an election and come back a few years later because nobody wants the job.

You can't?

Bill, you won't be able to raise a dime for another campaign! What about your pork bellies money?

Don't even think about it.

Chelsea's been saving, hasn't she?

Forget it, Bill. I've got it in a trust fund.

Okay, okay . . . well, listen. If I lose the presidency, can I at least run for governor again?

RECOVERING FROM SEXUAL SCANDAL

Well now, it's one thing to have the missus find out that Little Elvis has been on tour. A heartfelt apology, a diamond necklace, the promise of a Supreme Court appointment, and soon this tiny bump in the road of marriage is forgotten. It's quite another thing, though, to have the whole world listening to a tape of you on the phone with a Stuckey's waitress telling her that you're absolutely positive the penicillin worked and it's probably some perfectly natural discharge. I mean, leaders of the Free World are people too. Despite our extraordinary stamina and size, we're only human, with human weaknesses. I don't have to tell you that Kennedy, Roosevelt and L.B.J. are all known to have dipped the wick. I've heard rumors about George Bush playing the occasional game of Hide the Oil Derrick in the Lincoln Bedroom. And if those inflatable penile implants had been perfected sooner, who knows what Ronald Reagan might have done during his daily hour of wakefulness? Did they get raked over the coals for it? No. But one or two hundred *alleged* indiscretions on my part and all of a sudden it's open season on young, charismatic Presidents. Well, I won't have any of it. It's not my fault. If my spirit and my will are in the hand of my Higher Power, then who knows what else of mine he's got in his other hand? Let he who is without sin cast the first stone. Sit down, Carter, or I'll belt you one.

Step Four. We Take Stock of Ourselves
Unsparingly and Take Note of Our Flaws, No
Matter How Tremendously Overshadowed
They Are by Our Stellar Qualities.

Now, this Step can be a difficult one. None of us likes to look at our flaws. But we must be merciless, because we are going to list our shortcomings for God—and He already knows them anyway. We can hide our flaws from ourselves, we can hide them from our spouses (sometimes for years if the goddamn press doesn't get involved), but there's no point in trying to hide them from God. As it says in the Bible, "He sees you when you're sleeping, He knows when you're awake, He knows if you've been bad or good, so be good for goodness's sake."

Here's an effective method I've found for taking stock of my flaws. I take a piece of scrap paper—we've got a huge stack of these "From the White House desk of LINDA BLOODWORTH-THOMASON" pads in one of the supply closets—and I fold it down the middle as if I were making a paper airplane. At the top of the left side, I write, "President Bill Clinton—Strengths"; on the right side, I write "President Bill Clinton—Flaws." Before I begin, I take a good long look at the paper, breathing deeply, thinking about what I've done as President, what remains undone, where my strengths have helped me and where my flaws have held me back. I remember that there's no room here for personal vanity, that this is no time for playing fast and loose with the facts—that right now, at this moment, even if I have never done so before in my life, *it is absolutely critical that I come up with nothing but the pure, unvarnished truth.* Then I give the paper to Hillary and let her fill it out.

I can usually get it done inside of two minutes. Front and back.

You *could* take a little more time with the "Strengths" column.

RECOVERING FROM GETTING A HUGE WENDY'S KETCHUP STAIN OR YOUR TIE RIGHT BEFORE THE STATE OF THE UNION ADDRESS

"Goddamn these stupid little packets, there's no goddamn way to open them without the ketchup getting all over your goddamn clothes! I'm gonna tax that Dave Thomas son of a bitch until the Big Bacon Classic sprouts legs, gets down on its knees and begs for mercy!" I guess we've all said similar things at one time or another after a condiment mishap. But a situation like this—screwing up our appearance just before a live speech on worldwide television, solely because of our own gluttony—is a perfect opportunity to *let the past go*. Sure, if I'd restrained my appetite for one lousy hour, I'd be going out there to face the American public with the bearing of a visionary ready to lead the nation into the next century, instead of looking like a fat country-boy slob who's never met the business end of a napkin. But what's done is done. No use blaming myself; now it's time to deal maturely with the situation. Stephanopoulos! Get over here and give me your tie.

Step Five. We Tell God Everything That's Wrong with Ourselves, and Ask Him How Much of It Is Likely to Come Out During the Campaign.

As I mentioned in Step Four, God already knows our flaws. We're only listing them as a courtesy to Him, the way you'd let Gore sit in on a policy meeting. But just as you have to give Gore one of the comfortable chairs like everyone else, and not put him on the footstool over by the ficus, so you must present God with the most complete and unblinking assessment you can muster of your flaws. It means a certain amount of discomfort—nobody wants to listen to Hairspray Boy whine about the ozone layer when we're brainstorming over the approval rating, and nobody wants to look bad in the eyes of our Higher Power— but it's necessary if we are to work our way through to recovery.

Now, there's an upside to all this soul-searching. God knows everything, right? So maybe, seeing how sincere we are about recovering and all, he wants to help us out a little by letting us in on which of these slight flaws of ours is likely to surface during the campaign. I mean, if I'd known in 1992 that Gennifer Flowers was going to open her big fat—I mean, that unsubstantiated allegations of infidelity would be floated by unscrupulous Republican tricksters, I might have been better prepared when the poo-poo hit the fan. God could have done that for me, if He'd wanted to. And I feel confident that He *will* do it for me next time, if anyone should get wind of that business with the Barbi twins . . .

I tell you what, too. As soon as God starts advising me, the very first time he speaks to me, you know who I'm gonna tell about it? That's right: Her Worship, Jimmy Carter. I can't wait to see Carter's big bug eyes get all watery and sad. Guy thinks he's got a personal cel phone to the Lord.

I know that this Step—Confessing your worst faults to God— can appear very daunting to some people. I'd just like to take this moment to urge you to forget your fears and jump right in. Do it! You'll feel better. I found the act of telling God everything that's wrong with me to be quite cleansing. It was over very quickly, but it was exhilarating while it lasted.

What did you tell Him?

That's between me and God, isn't it? But I can give you a hint: It had something to do with my taste in men.

RECOVERING FROM A CONFLICT OF INTEREST SCANDAL

My fellow Americans, what do you do for a living? Do you work for a small business or a large corporation? Maybe you get company discounts on merchandise, or even free products, and maybe you trade those products to friends in exchange for free products that they receive? Or perhaps you are an entrepreneur, running your own small store or auto repair shop. Maybe your friend the butcher comes to your garage with some bad struts, and with Easter coming and all, you agree to replace his struts in exchange for a nice crown roast. Do you think you deserve to be the target of a Congressional investigation?

No, of course not. Well, my business is governing. And if I should happen to trade some of the perquisites of my business—a tax abatement instead of a set of struts, a squashed indictment instead of a crown roast—why should I be treated any differently? Whitewater was a simple case of a nice couple, Hillary and myself, getting caught in a bad investment and then making an honest attempt to turn it around. You'd do the same thing if you were in our shoes. If you were Governor and your wife was an attorney and you both had a financial stake in a real estate venture managed by a savings and loan company which she represented before the State Securities Commission and whose majority owner you appointed as one of your liaisons to the State Senate despite evidence of questionable loan activity on the part of a bank he ran before selling it to buy the thrift whose subsidiary managed the development project. I believe you'd do exactly what we did. Which was give up trying to figure the whole thing out and get the hell into commodity futures.

Step Six. We Tell God We're Ready to Have Him Remove All Defects of Character, and Humbly Ask His Permission to Leak the Good News.

This is the second really crucial Step, the "other shoe" to Step Three. In that Step, we made the decision to turn our lives over to our Higher Power. In this Step, having made that decision, we respectfully let our Higher Power in on where we want to go with this deal. You might think it's contradictory to turn my will over to the Lord and then start telling Him what to do with it. Well, I see your point and you're absolutely right. But this is politics, damn it, not the Garden of Eden, and if God wants to play, He has to play hardball.

Besides, I'm doing Him a favor. God is very busy, and I'm just trying to streamline the decision-making process for Him so He doesn't make an administrative mistake. I mean, what if I turn my will and my life over to God, and He decides, "Well, heck, this guy says it's all up to me—he looks like he'd make an excellent guinea pig for this new flesh-eating bacteria I've been developing down in the workshop"? Next thing I know I'm trying to sign a health bill into law and my skin is falling off and getting all over the paper and Dole, instead of standing there holding back tears, is laughing his ass off. Does that seem very presidential to you? Huh?

My friends, I can't let that happen. I began preparing myself for public service when I was still a boy in Arkansas. I went to Oxford. I went to Yale Law. I spent five terms—*five terms!*—as governor of a state so poor that every Halloween, African children sent us *their* UNICEF money. You think it's fun being the chief executive of a state that's forty percent chickens, sixty percent chicken shit?

Bill . . .

Don't misinterpret me; I love Arkansas and Arkansans. Those years wasted governing yokels and yahoos were some of the best times of my life. All I'm saying is, I paid my dues. Of course I'm *happy* to turn my life and my will over to God. He is the greatest force in my life, after all, and the source of my deep-seated commitment to blah blah blah blah blah. But I want Him to understand that it's just not in the cards for me to go back to the South after one term and build outhouses like some other presidents I could name. You've got my will, You've got my life, now remove my defects of character and let's go out there and win this thing. That's all I'm saying. Make me a better man, a better president, and then let me get on the horn to Peter Jennings and let him know about it. Or better yet, if You can spare the time, it would have a lot more impact coming from You. Appear to him in a dream or something. Maybe as a burning bush? Aw, heck, I'll leave it up to You, You'll come up with something much better than I could.

Bill is right about the importance of this Step. Life is funny. A person can be born blessed with a high degree of intelligence, a true gift for communicating with his fellow man, a genuine passion to do what is right. And for all that, he can still be kept from reaching greatness by a few small, nearly insignificant character flaws. An insulting lack of discrimination about where his penis ends up, for instance. Or the decision-making capabilities of a three-year-old choosing between ice cream and cake. Or a slavish need for approval rarely seen outside the world of dogs. So if you do happen to be a person like that, it really is important to ask God to get rid of these flaws, on the wafer-thin chance that in the waning days of your term you might, for once in your big-talking, smoke-blowing life, actually be able to get something done.

You're speaking hypothetically, right?

Of course, darling.

RECOVERING FROM A VISIT BY
BARBRA STREISAND

Put the furniture back the way it was before she came over and, if possible, repaint the walls their original color. Rescind the Cabinet appointments she made and put your own people back in the jobs. Cancel the trade agreements she signed and restore the tax code to what it was yesterday. Abort the flights of any ICBMs she has launched or, if that is not possible, call target nations and offer apologies.

Step Seven. We Respectfully Ask Him to Get It Done Before the New Hampshire Primary.

No mystery about this Step. I can't do much for our nation if the Lord doesn't get around to my recovery 'til 1997, can I? No, a deity that created the world in seven days can certainly manage to remove my few flaws by February. Hell, it's probably an outpatient procedure.

If He really gets done that quickly, perhaps you should ask Him if He'd mind excising some other people's flaws too.

Other people?

It might be easier to work with Jesse Helms, for instance, if you eliminated his rigidity and his self-righteousness and his vindictiveness and his bitterness and his short-sightedness and his stubbornness.

Whoa. You're asking God to do a lot there.

Well, most of Helms's problems seem to be centered in his pysche. Maybe God can get rid of them quickly by just removing his head.

RECOVERING FROM A STUPID
MANAGEMENT SCANDAL

I don't know what state you're from, but down in Arkansas it's sometimes kind of hard to know who's a relative and who isn't. People don't like to travel very far to find a spouse, and down the hall to Sis's room is often as big a trip as they'll make. And with my mother having been married four times that she could remember, and half-brothers and half-sisters popping up all over the place like mushrooms, it's especially difficult to keep track of the family tree in my own case. I mean, after a while you just sort of assume that everyone's related to you in one way or another. So when I fired half the White House travel office and put my own cousin in charge, I knew it might look bad, but I reasoned that anybody I put in would eventually turn out to be my cousin anyway. You see? Your President is always thinking ahead. I hope that gives you a feeling of confidence.

***Step Eight. We Make a List of Political
Enemies We've Made and Determine Their
Influence in Congress, the Media and
the Public Arena.***

The crucial question with this Step is, how far back do we go with it? In 1969 I pulled a low draft number and then wrote to the Arkansas ROTC commander to tell him I'd changed my mind about joining the program. If I'd known then that I was pissing off a guy who'd still be around to talk about it in 1992, I would have sent a fruit basket or something along with the letter to smooth things over.

The point is, it's a bad idea to rush this Step. Take as much time as you need to make sure you don't miss anybody. Go through your Rolodex. Check your official correspondence. Review your cancelled checks. Look over your phone bill. Read your love letters, if the ife-way is out of the ouse-hay. Go down your list of withdrawn Cabinet

appointments. Flip through your high school yearbook. Browse through your subpoenas. Examine your file of staffers who have resigned in disgrace. Look over the list of incumbent Democrats defeated in 1994— I don't care how long it takes. You'll be amazed at how the names pile up.

I should have mentioned to have plenty of paper and sharpened pencils on hand before you start. Also get a good night's sleep first and take some vitamins. A checkup isn't a bad idea either.

While you're at it, don't forget to check your list of betrayed spouses.

Heh heh. You're funny, Hillary.

Heh heh.

RECOVERING FROM THAT HORRY OLD TENT PREACHER JIMMY CARTER GETTING ALL THE GOOD PRESS

W hen I was a child, attending grade school in Arkansas, there was a little boy in the class who had the nickname "Take A Bow Billy." Any time the students of the school achieved something positive, this youngster was somehow there to take credit—even when he had nothing to do with it. When the Parents' Association announced how much money was raised at the bake sale, he managed to be there with his hands full of flour. When the students instituted a program of doing chores for the elderly, he managed to be on the podium to receive the principal's congratulations. When the fifth-grade class won the Arkansas Governor's Special Achievement Award because almost half the children could read the word "Exit" above the door, he managed to get his picture in the local newspaper.

What does this have to do with Jimmy Carter? I think you know by now—for my friends, "Take a Bow Billy" was myself. And it really pisses me off that Jimmy Carter thinks he can horn in on my act just because he keeps flying around the world stopping wars that I've started. True, my fate and my future are in the hands of my Higher Power, and it is a counterproductive waste of time for me to have these negative feelings. But my Higher Power tells me that if I invite old "Roids" Carter to a White House dinner and have the toilet paper impregnated with cayenne pepper, I'll feel a lot better about the whole thing.

Step Nine. We Kiss Up to as Many of Those People as Possible and Promise Appointments to the Rest.

The great thing about this Step is that it finally gives us something to *do*. I mean, once you've turned your life and your will over to God and asked Him to handle everything from here on out, that doesn't leave much on the old Presidential schedule for you, does it? But with this step, you're getting on the phone brown-nosing legislators and party bigwigs and labor leaders and lobbyists and reporters and contributors . . . Man, it's like the good old days back in Arkansas, except now everybody takes my call and nobody ever says, "I told you already I have a fiance stationed in Germany, and if you phone me again I'm calling the police." Plus I've got something now that I didn't have back then: White House stationery. Mounds and mounds of White House stationery. Nothing smooths over ruffled feathers like a personalized note on White House stationery—except a personalized note on White House stationery that says, "I'd like you to head up the White House travel office." See, when you've really pissed somebody off, past the point where a fruit basket will have any effect, you reach for the big guns: you offer them a government job.

I know what you're thinking. You're saying, "How often can you pull that one? There are only a finite number of positions to go around." I see your point and you're absolutely right. In fact, you'll recall that my mother said something very similar to my Daddy the night I was conceived. But we're not talking about sex here, we're talking about presidential appointments, and what does one have to do with the other? Don't answer that.

Just a little Chief Executive humor there. You're saying there are only so many *jobs* available in the federal government. True enough. But I'm not talking about putting people in those jobs. I'm talking about *promising* to put people in those jobs. I stumbled on this technique by accident when I first ran for governor of Arkansas. During the campaign I scoured the state looking for the hundred people best qualified to run the government, and I offered each of them a position. Once I was in office I found there were fewer jobs than I'd been led to believe, so some of those hundred people had to be disappointed—about ninety of them, actually. I felt bad for a couple of hours, but I managed to bounce back. I mean, the election was over, after all. Besides, I drew comfort from my philosophy studies at Oxford, where I'd learned Martin Heidegger's famous theorem: "It's the thought that counts." I think that was Heidegger. It might have been Hegel.

Anyway, in the federal government, of course, there are hundreds of thousands of jobs, which means you can promise them to millions of people. Tens of millions of people, for that matter. Actually, I suppose if you took this approach to its extreme, you could theoretically promise a job to every voter in the country. Ha ha ha ha, I gotta tell that one to Hillary. She'll get a laugh out of it. Hey, Hillary! Hilla— Wait a minute.

My fellow Americans, I'm pleased to take this opportunity to make a historic announcement about governmental responsiveness and accountability: From now on I can guarantee you that your federal government will absolutely reflect your wishes and desires, because I am going to appoint each and every one of you to a post in the Clinton Administration! That is correct. Right after the election in November 1996, each of you will receive notification by mail of your new position. Congratulations on this prestigious and well-earned appointment.

Bill, I've said it before, but it bears repeating. You're good. You're damn good.

Thank you, dear.

RECOVERING FROM A PSYCHO FIRING SHOTS INTO THE WHITE HOUSE DINING ROOM AT TWO IN THE MORNING

Every President must live with the knowledge that at any moment he could be the target of an assassin's bullet, and I am resigned to that possibility. Even so, it's a little disconcerting to realize that you can't even enjoy a routine snack without worrying about security. I mean, with all the rooms upon rooms in the White House, how'd he ever figure out that I'd be in the dining room? *How did he know?* I guess that question will haunt me forever.

Anyway, working with the Secret Service, I have devised a schedule that divides my daily meals equally among three places: the dining room, the White House pantry and my private quarters. Since I will now be in the dining room only six or seven times a day, I will be far less vulnerable to attack.

RECOVERING FROM A PSYCHO FIRING SHOTS INTO THE WHITE HOUSE PRESS ROOM AT TWO IN THE AFTERNOON

Pardon me if I'm dense, but I've been over it and over it and I just don't see how this is a problem.

Step Ten. We Keep Making Lists of Everything Wrong With Us, on the Slim Chance That We'll Be Ready the Next Time the Media Unearths Something We Did in the '80s.

All right, I know it's a long shot, but sometimes it works. For instance: In Arkansas, the license plates on the Governor's limousine traditionally read AK-1. One year, an old buddy from Arkansas calls me up to say that he and some of the chicken boys are going out to blow off a little steam, and would I like to tag along? We decided to make a night of it, and we thought we'd look more, you know, impressive in the big official car. No big deal, we chipped in for gas. The next day I don't remember much, I'm pretty hung over, and when I get into the limo for the ride to work, the license plates read LUVMOBILE. Well, it was a good joke, and I got the official plates back on before Hillary returned from her conference. Good, clean fun. But see, if the press got ahold of that, I just *know* they'd blow it all out of proportion, and they'd dig up those two aerobics instructors we gave a lift home, and who knows, maybe find the jojoba oil and the video and stuff, and before you know it I'd have a whole new problem on my hands.

But thanks to the Twelve Steps, I remembered those LUVMOBILE license plates, made a few calls and they're gone for good. Now no one will ever know they existed. Er, except you readers, I guess. Oh. Yeah. Uh, do me a favor and don't say anything about this.

LUVMOBILE? You rode around the state with plates reading LUVMOBILE?

Sure, I told you about that, honey, remember? When we went to the couples workshop? You said you'd forgive and forget. I guess you did, ha ha ha.

We never went to a couples workshop.

Oops, you're right. Well, you can see it was a harmless prank, can't you?

Sure.

Thanks, honey.

Who'd you go with to the couples workshop?

RECOVERING FROM LEAKS

When we were kids and the juvenile narcotics squad would knock down the front door and drag him out kicking and screaming, my brother Roger used to shout "Nobody likes a snitch!" over his shoulder at me just before they stuffed him in the back of the police car. Now, say what you want about Roger, but he had a point. When you tell somebody something in confidence, like for instance about how you plan to add a modest ten-thousand percent tax increase to finance your new health care package, and then they go and blab that to Peter "Tsk Tsk" Jennings, well, it just isn't right. But my Higher Power has shown me a simple way to keep my legislative agenda from being leaked to the press before I'm ready to announce it: If I don't *have* any agenda, then there's nothing to leak! This new direction will give me a chance to kick back and get some well-deserved rest, too. No plans, no goals, no struggling. I got the idea from reviewing the accomplishments of the Bush Administration. Hmm, that wily old George must have gone through recovery too!

Step Eleven. We Keep Trying to Get on God's Good Side. And Everyone Else's Too, Except Those Pricks Gingrich and Dole, Who Don't Have One.

You may have noticed that in the Program up to now, there's been a lot of asking God for things and not a whole lot of giving things back to Him. Well, if you've got an election coming up and you're going to need His help, it's time to show Him a little concrete appreciation.

This presents a bit of a problem. I mean, what can *you* possibly give *God*? It's not like you're going to impress him with a fruit basket. That's like surprising Dave Thomas on his birthday with a Wendy's Half-Pound Double and Large Frosty: He makes the damn things every day, chances are you'll just end up eating them yourself, and you already pulled that trick on Him last year.

What to give, then? Political patronage? I don't think God is really interested in being an Undersecretary of Labor, do you? Cash won't work, and a gift certificate's out of the question—it would require redeeming, and if He's going to show Himself, it'll be to do something spectacular like part the Red Sea, not to pick out a sweater at the Gap.

No, I've been pondering this question, really chewing it over. In fact I've assembled a task force to consider it, and we've all come to the same conclusion: the ancient religions had it right. God wants sacrifice. That's right, He wants some blood spilled. He gets off on it.

Once again, you're wondering about the logic in this. If God made all creatures, wouldn't killing any of them anger Him?

Bulletin: God has a bad day now and then, just like the rest of us. And when He has a bad day, He can't rely on the Supreme Court or his wife or Panetta to clean up the mess. He's all alone with His mistakes—and that's our opportunity to serve Him. Not by sacrificing one of his beautiful innocent creatures like a lamb, but by getting rid of a few of his glaring mistakes for him. Some of his real howlers. I think we all know what I'm talking about.

Like let's say you're God, and You're bored one day, and You think it would stir things up if You worked it so that all these idiots and reactionaries with absolutely no legislative experience were suddenly elected to the House of Representatives. So You do that, and things *are* interesting for a while, until they start talking about building orphanages and putting assault weapons back on the street and constructing space bombs and stuff and You think, whoa, this isn't such a good joke anymore. But what do You do about it?

You turn to one of Your most devoted servants, that's what. I can help. I've got all these CIA operatives sitting around with nothing to do, and your average Congress-person has absolutely no idea how to spot the warning signs of curare poisoning. Let me at 'em, Lord. It's the least I can do to demonstrate my appreciation for Your help.

Term limits? I'll show the bastards some term limits.

Bill, this is the one Step in the program I'm having a little trouble with. I just don't see why I should have to grovel to God. I mean, She knows everything, so therefore She knows how hard I've been working for the good of the American people, right? I don't want to overstep my bounds here, but it seems to me that if God had done Her job correctly in the first place as regards the human body, I wouldn't have to be working so hard on health care and children's rights. I've actually got some proposals to bring up to God, vis-a-vis an improved immune system and built-in contraceptive mechanism, and I bet after I make my presentation God will be trying to get on *my* good side. But that's okay, I'm willing to work with Her. Because the key to my relationship with God, above all else, is humility.

RECOVERING FROM YOUR VICE PRESIDENT BEING SMARTER THAN YOU

Hey, so what? Brains aren't everything. Did you ever notice how these egghead types are always real drips? Real stiff, no sense of humor, always trying to bring you down when you want to do a little partying. And it's not just Hillary. Gore is that way too. But she thought, you know, if we had somebody like him on board it would bring up the administration's average SAT scores all around, and I'm not sure but I think Tipper promised to go shopping for makeup with her too. Meanwhile I'm figuring, the guy's a dead ringer for Clark Kent, a certain percentage of the voters are going to think they're electing Superman. I heard from a good source that Dan Quayle voted for us for that reason. So go ahead, Al, talk about the ozone layer and the rain forest and stuff all you want. And listen, would you and Tipper mind inviting Hillary to one of your Scrabble games tonight? I've got, uh, a debriefing to attend.

Step Twelve: We Carry Our Message of Redemption and Re-Election to Others Through Sound Bites, Photo Ops and the Occasional Interminable Speech.

This is my favorite Step of all. We've got a name for this Step where I come from, and the name is good old-fashioned campaigning. It's great to be back in the saddle! My fellow Americans, God's fixing me up! Let me tell you about it! And since the message I bring comes directly from God, I think it's only fair that you TV people give me some free airtime with which to explain it! Yeah, come on, America, let me tell you my story of redemption and recovery! And let me tell it to you without dipping into the old war chest!

That's how it's gonna be. Bring on 1996! Man, I feel good. I feel ready. I've completed the Twelve Steps and I know I can govern this great land like it's never been governed before. Hello, world, it's me, Bill Clinton, and I'm gonna make you love me! Yes I will! Yes I will! Don't tell me not to march, my heart's a drummer! Hey Mister Arnstein, here I am!

Bill, what are these pills I found on the night-stand?

Oh, I got those at over at Bethesda. I told the doctor I was feeling a little blue. They're called Prozac.

Your doctor prescribed Prozac?

Not *my* doctor, exactly. I met this other doctor there.

You "met" another doctor at Bethesda?

Not *at* Bethesda, exactly. He works out of his car in the garage there. He says half of Congress is using this stuff. He told me he used to prescribe something else, but it made Bush blow lunch all over the Japanese prime minister.

Bill . . . are you sure this man is on the government payroll?

Well, he will be. I'm thinking about naming him Surgeon General.

RECOVERING FROM HAVING TO BEG REPUBLICAN LEGISLATORS FOR SUPPORT

Occasionally a top advisor will ask me, "How can you stand to swallow your pride day in and day out, spending all your time begging votes from people who want nothing more than to humiliate you?" My answer is always the same. "Listen, Hillary," I say, "you better than anyone should know that I'm used to begging." But the truth is more complicated than that. See, Dole thinks he's really put one over on you when he makes you sacrifice your dignity and come crawling to him for votes. He gets off on it. In fact, I have it on good authority from someone who knew Elizabeth at Transportation that it's the only time he can land the 747 in the old hangar anymore, if you know what I mean.

Now my friends, growing up as close to my mother as I did, I saw the damage that can be inflicted by a marriage in crisis. And another marriage in crisis. And a couple more. So if my Higher Power has chosen me as the starch to put a little stiffness into the Doles's bedroom, well, hell, I don't mind a bit of groveling and crawling for a good cause. I just keep thinking of Nelson Rockefeller, and how he died of a heart attack in bed ramming home his final piece of legislation, so to speak, and I think, hey, maybe lightning will strike twice. Besides, I'd sure want someone to do the same for me if Little Elvis suddenly decided to cancel all personal appearances. (Not that he shows any signs of cutting back his schedule!) It's all part of my recovery. Besides, I've got a secret Dole doesn't know about: he can't force me to swallow my pride. I don't *have* any pride.

RECOVERING FROM HAVING TO BEG DEMOCRATIC LEGISLATORS FOR SUPPORT

I just pretend they're Republicans. Hillary says everyone in Congress, the Pentagon, and the press are all against us anyway. She's been mumbling a lot lately and tugging at her hair. Should I be worried?

RECOVERING FROM HAVING TO BEG A STUCKEY'S WAITRESS FOR SUPPORT

You know what really ticks me off? I'm supposed to be the Chief Executive, right? There's supposed to be a little respect that goes along with that, right? I mean maybe not in Washington, where no one is impressed with anything. But when you get into a helicopter with the Presidential Seal on it, and your decorated Navy pilot flies it up to Atlantic City with a two-helicopter escort and sets that baby down smack in the middle of a cordoned-off Stuckey's parking lot, and the Secret Service descends on the place like locusts, and after it's all secure you go marching in there like God, look around the place, and crook your finger at a know-nothing, white-trash waitress barely out of her

teens—I mean, you'd expect that girl to *jump*, wouldn't you? Instead of cracking her gum and saying, "I have to meet my boyfriend." Man. When I say I'm concerned about the direction of America's youth, that's not simply rhetoric, my friends. Anyway, just promise her she can attend a White House dinner with Brad Pitt and your problems are over. Like I'd ever invite Brad Pitt to the White House along with a chick. I'm not an idiot, you know.

Chapter Seven

A NOTE ABOUT GOD AS
WE UNDERSTAND HIM

As I mentioned in the last chapter, one of our most cherished American freedoms is the right to worship—or *not* to worship—as we please. I realize that a certain percentage of the American public consider themselves to be atheists, and as a freedom-loving American President, I respect and defend their right to do so. Particularly since you *know* they're not going to be Republicans, so they're all potential votes. (You atheist kids just go ahead and use that "moment of silence" in the schools to work on your twelves table or something. Ignore the threats from the other children.)

Still, you're wondering. How can I, as a freedom-of-worship-supporting President, put forth a Twelve-Step program that appears to rely heavily on a concept of God?

My answer is to ask you to carefully reread Step Three, which states that my Bible Belt upbringing taught me to call the Higher Power, God. You may have another name for the Higher Power, and that's fine. Krishna, or Chuck or something. Or you may not believe in a Higher Power at all, but only in an ideal standard of behavior that you strive for. If you feel uncomfortable calling that ideal God, that's fine. Add an "o" to God and call it Good. You can accept an abstract idea of Good, can't you? It's interesting to see what a change one letter can make. Change an "e" to a "t" and you get Dolt. Bob Dolt. Senate Majority Leader Bob Dolt. Bob and Elizabeth, the Dolts. Jimmy Farter. Vice President El Bore. I'd like to order a Happy Feel, please. I could go on and on.

Anyway, a Higher Power means whatever *your* image of a Higher Power is. Maybe it's the traditional bearded God, or Jesus, or Buddha. For myself, when I sit down and really try to envision the deity, I get a strange picture in my head. It's some sort of multidimensional being, existing simultaneously on different levels, with a nurturing softness at the highest, lowest and middle planes. Alternating with that soft, nurturing force is a darker, tougher kind of material, with a distinct life-energy to it. And there's some sort of ectoplasmic ooze keeping these different forces apart. And some old lettuce.

Bill, I think you just described a Big Mac.

Hey, you're right! What about you, Hillary? Tell the people what you see when you think of God.

Well, I picture God in the more traditional human form, I suppose. She's got a no-nonsense air about Her, and you can tell She means business—She really wants to run the universe well—and maybe some people interpret that as being standoffish, even though She's just the opposite. She really cares about people and their problems, but somehow She gets all this bad publicity for not being Betty Crocker or Donna Reed or something. That's just sort of the way I picture Her.

Does She have a daughter named Chelsea?

What?

Nothing.

RECOVERING FROM A FAILED
CABINET APPOINTMEAT

You know, when you're President, people are always trying to take perfectly reasonable actions and turn them into big deals. Let's say you, Mr. or Ms. American Citizen, had to find a plumber to fix a stopped-up kitchen sink. How would you go about it? Most likely you'd ask around, talk to your friends and neighbors, get a couple of recommendations. Okay, you call the most promising candidate, he comes over, says, "Sure, I can fix your sink." Then while he's underneath it, banging around with the wrenches and stuff, are you really going to crouch down and say, "By the way, Charlie, you don't have an illegal alien watching your children right now, do you?"

No. You don't have to ask him that. You're not a public servant, so you're allowed a little privacy. You don't have Peter Jennings calling up your household staff every morning asking if they found any interesting hairs on the sheets today. But I, the President of the United States, *do* have to make these inquiries. And even if Charlie says, "Yes, right now my kids are with a crippled old woman whose legs were ruined by thirty years of torture in a Cuban prison, all for saying 'God Bless President Eisenhower,'" you have to let him go, no matter if the goddamn sink is overflowing like Niagara Falls. Because he's broken the law. So a good man is cheated out of an honest day's work, and meanwhile the sink is still gushing, and you absentmindedly brush up against it pouring yourself a glass of water. And when you go down to the Capitol Building to lobby for your crime bill, Dole is snickering and cracking jokes to his buddies about how the President better appropriate some funding to replenish the White House supply of Depends.

Now, I understand that an Attorney General is not a plumber (except in the Nixon White House, heh heh). The Attorney General is supposed to uphold and enforce the laws of the land, and shouldn't be breaking them at home. Fair enough. Zoe Baird wasn't right for the job. I accepted that, and, like you'd do with the plumber, I went to my second choice. Turns out Kimba Wood also had nanny problems. Okay, fine. So again, I did what you'd do at this point: I grabbed the yellow pages and looked under L for Lady Lawyers, and eventually I came up with somebody. My point is, if I don't criticize you for the way you pick your plumber, I don't see where you get off criticizing me for picking my Cabinet the same way.

RECOVERING FROM A SLIGHT MISJUDGMENT IN THE USE OF DEADLY FORCE

This is what always happens when you hire somebody out of the yellow pages. Okay, there's this insane David Koresh guy who thinks he's God come to earth as a rock star, holed up in a compound with all these white-trash idiots who believe in him. Man, what I could do with a few million registered voters like that. Anyway, this nut is forcing a showdown, and Janet Reno wants to know what she should do about it. Just leave him in there until his medication kicks in and he comes out peacefully, or surround the place, cut off food and water, bombard it with light and noise for a few weeks and finally overrun it with commandos?

Now, think about it for a minute. At this point the presidency is already going not so good, and here I've been on several talk shows, playing my saxophone in dark glasses and reminiscing about how when I was younger I wanted to be Elvis. You see my problem here? If I don't come down on this Koresh guy, people are going to begin talking about how maybe it's because he reminds me of myself. I mean, Christ, with my family history, I wouldn't be surprised if they started digging and found out he was my half-brother or something—and I already *have* a burnt-out half-brother with delusions of rock stardom, thank you very much. Not that I don't love and stand by the parasite one hundred percent, don't get me wrong, but I need another Roger in my life like I need another "can't miss" real estate deal.

So I tell Reno to go ahead and do what she thinks is best, and you know how qualified *she* is. I don't have to remind you what happened next. It wasn't exactly Rescue at Entebbe.

What's my point? Well, if you people had let me go with Zoe Baird as Attorney General in the first place, none of this might have happened. But let's put that behind us. I want to pledge here and now that in my next term, I'll work hard to come up with the very best people for Cabinet positions, if *you'll* promise to be a little more tolerant in your reaction to them. And even though I know I shouldn't, I want to "leak" one of those exciting appointments planned for my second term. While keeping my promise to have a woman in the post, I'll be naming a brilliant new Attorney General: Lani Guinier.

Chapter Eight

I'M WITH STUPID

A SPECIAL CHAPTER ON
RECOVERING FROM
RELATIONSHIP MISTAKES

I hope you don't mind if at this point I diverge a bit from our program of political recovery to talk about *relationship* recovery. Now, I'm no marriage counselor, that's for sure.

That would be like Ross Perot giving stress management workshops.

Yes, well, thank you very much, dear. My point is that when there is dysfunction in any area of our lives, it is bound to spill over into our principal relationship; and, correspondingly, recovering from problems in our relationship may help us recover from some of the other problems we have too. The most vital thing we can learn to do is keep our *work* life and our *home* life separate. Do you agree, Hillary?

Absolutely. When you've set aside time to be with your significant other, absolutely nothing should—Ah, hell, there goes my beeper again. I'll be right back.

What Hillary means is, let's say you come home from the office at night and you're a little wound up from the job. Maybe you gave somebody at work an ultimatum, someone who should respect your words, and instead he laughed in your face and kept right on shelling Sarajevo. And you go home feeling, well, maybe I'm not master of my

work situation, but at least I can be master of my own home. And you walk in the door and say, "Woman, where's my dinner?" And instead of "Coming right up, nice and hot," you get, "Where's *your* dinner? I spent the whole day fighting off drug manufacturers threatening to take their jobs to Switzerland over the health bill! Where's *my* dinner?" That's when the two of you need some candles, a rose in a vase, a glass of wine and some cuddle time to remember that you are the most important people in each other's lives.

Whoa! Sorry! I'm back! Now where the hell did I put those goddamn Health and Human Services numbers from the GAO? Shit!

Of course, sometimes the best way to deal with a tense spouse is to give them their space. Get away by yourself for a quick cup of coffee. Go to Stuckey's or somewhere.

RECOVERING FROM A STAFF REORGANISATION

Change is good. When people stay in the same job for too long, they become stale. Er, I don't mean Presidents. I mean other kinds of people. So there's nothing wrong with taking, say, your communications director and making him your special assistant. Or taking Ronald Reagan's speech writer and making him your special counselor. Or cutting loose your Deputy Treasury Secretary and your Secretary of Agriculture because of a few bad decisions involving real estate and chickens. Or firing your Surgeon General after she comes out in favor of flogging the dolphin. The important thing is that these changes are not made hastily, but deliberately, after much reflection and soul-searching. As I said, change is good, so long as it is change born of thought and planning, not political decisions arrived at in a panic.

RECOVERING FROM ANOTHER STAFF REORGANISATION OF THE NEXT DAY

Hey, you never made a mistake?

Chapter Nine

RECOVERY DREAMS

Here's a little tip on how to monitor the progress of your recovery. Trying to gauge it yourself is almost impossible, because you're likely to get distracted by petty issues and self-delusions. But the subconscious never lies, which is one reason I'm glad I don't talk in my sleep. By writing down our dreams as soon as we awaken and then carefully analyzing them, we can see if we are moving toward a state of mental health and happiness, or instead heading down the Ted Kennedy Highway.

For instance, I have this dream where I'm being chased down a long, dark corridor by a horrible creature. It's some kind of zombie or something, with this monstrous face, as if all the evil in his soul had settled on it and turned him into a chalk-skinned, flesh-eating ghoul. And try as I may to get away from him, I can't. He's pursuing me, and getting closer, and somehow I know that when he catches me he's going to devour me, slowly, tearing off chunk after chunk of my flesh with his teeth and laughing as he swallows each bite . . .

Is this monster carrying around a copy of the Washington Post, turned to an article about your low approval rating?

Yeah! How did you know?

That's not a flesh-eating ghoul, Bill. It's Dole.

Wow! You had the same dream?

No. I have my own recurring nightmare. I dream that I went

to bed, just the way I really did. But then it's morning, and I wake up to discover I'm wearing this gingham apron! I tug and tug at it with my left hand, but no matter what I do I can't get it off! And I want to use my right hand, too, but for some reason I can't, and then I realize it's because my right hand is holding a wooden spoon and stirring a big bowl of cookie dough! That's when I wake up screaming.

Wow! That *is* scary! What do you think it means?

Well, the apron and the cookie dough are traditional symbols of domesticity. So I think it means my domestic policy work is starting to stifle me and it's time I assumed a bigger role in foreign policy.

Excuse me for a second, dear. I thought I heard Stephanopoulos calling for a glass of water.

RECOVERING FROM GETTING A HAIRCUT AT A HIRE, PLACE AND PRICE THAT IN RETROSPECT SEEMS LIKE MAYBE IT WASN'T SUCH A GREAT IDEA

As you know, the people of Russia are engaged in a historic struggle to establish a stable democracy, and we support and applaud them in that effort. It wasn't too long ago, however, that the Russians were caught in the yoke of a totalitarian entity known as the Soviet Union—a cruel, dehumanizing place where freedom was systematically quashed. Now. If you open up a history book and look at pictures of the last thirty or forty years of Russian leaders, what is it that you see?

Bad hair.

Yes, bad hair. Khrushchev. Kosygin. Brezhnev. Each one sporting hair clearly cut by a barber with no competition and no incentive to stay up-to-date on the latest styles—because in a totalitarian regime, the state, not the marketplace, controls the quality of haircuts.

Now look at our leaders' hair during the same period. J.F.K., L.B.J., Nixon. Forget Nixon. Ford, Carter, Reagan and Bush. No matter what look they chose, they had *quality* haircuts. The message they sent to our allies: Life is good in America. We have enough leisure time and disposable income to seek out well-trained, competent barbers. Overthrow your Communist chains and come get a styling.

My friends, an expensive haircut administered on an airport runway while thousands of travelers are forced to wait is no luxury for your President. It is an absolute necessity if I am to serve as a walking, talking advertisement for the glories of democracy. To those passengers who were inconvenienced, I ask you this: Which is a more sensible sacrifice to show the world the superiority of the democratic system— giving up your life on a cold battlefield in a distant land, or just giving up a couple of hours of your visit to Aunt Edna in Milwaukee?

Man, what a bunch of ingrates.

Chapter Ten

A PRESIDENTIAL
RECOVERY ROUND TABLE

It's been said that more people in my Administration have been through therapy than have served in the military. Well, let me just say this here and now. I never asked for an exemption from therapy. On the contrary, I was perfectly willing to put in my time in analysis, but it just so happened I was out of the country studying when the psychiatric draft—

Bill. Focus.

Okay. Sorry. What I meant to say was, in the great game of recovery, I'm the first to admit I'm playing catchup. But I believe we become great by studying greatness. Today, America is at an extraordinary point in her history—for we currently have four ex-presidents alive and willing to share their experience and wisdom with the country. I thought it might be beneficial to bring the four together to join Hillary and me in a discussion of how recovery has helped each of our Administrations. Here is a partial transcript of our conversation.

CLINTON: Each of you has had the honor of serving our Nation in its highest elective office.

CARTER: Ford was appointed.

CLINTON: True. But still, he knew the challenge of the presidency. And so—

CARTER: Yeah, but he's like the fella who marries his dead brother's fiancé. He didn't earn it.

FORD: Is that guy talking about me?

BUSH: Lighten up, Jimmy.

CARTER: Well, it's just that he got in the easy way.

REAGAN: So you lost your re-election campaign. Get over it.

BUSH: Yeah. *I* did.

REAGAN: You call what you had a campaign?

BUSH: What's that supposed to mean?

REAGAN: An election isn't like one of your Kenne-bunkport martinis, Prescott. You can't—

BUSH: I've asked you not to call me that.

REAGAN: —You can't just sit there in your wood-paneled library and wait for the butler to bring you the votes, Prescott.

BUSH: What the hell is eating you?

REAGAN: I'll tell you what's eating me. One word. Alzheimer's. I've got it. And I'm pissed.

FORD: Who's Alzheimlich? A Russian fella?

REAGAN: Jerry, when I lose control of my basic motor functions, I'll *still* have more on the ball than you.

CARTER: I admire your spirit, Ron. "Do not go gentle into that good night. Rage, rage against—"

REAGAN: Oh, shut up.

FORD: Could I have my check now? I'm teeing off in half an hour.

HILLARY: No check 'til we discuss recovery.

FORD: But I *always* get a check when I speak.

HILLARY: You haven't said anything yet. You hear me, Bill? No check.

REAGAN: What's the twist doing in here? I thought this was going to be stag.

CLINTON: Hillary is my most important and trusted advisor.

REAGAN: Yeah, that's what I used to say about Nancy—when she was in the room. Soon as she left, Meese and Deaver and I would unlock the secret desk drawer where I kept my old copies of *Rogue* and give 'em a look-see. Va-va-voom! You found that drawer yet, Bill?

BUSH: So *that's* what you did in the Oval Office. I knew there had to be something.

REAGAN: Aw, did I hurt your feelings, Prescott?

CARTER: I wonder if we could move the discussion to a higher plane. Talk about some of the things we've done since *leaving* office—

REAGAN, BUSH and CLINTON: Oh, shut up.

FORD: Cash would be fine, too.

REAGAN: Goddammit, you're stupid, Jerry.

HILLARY: Ask them about the endorsement, Bill.

CLINTON: Ah, I was wondering, since this discussion has really pointed up how much common ground we share, whether any of you would be interested in maybe endorsing me in the coming election. I mean since I've sought out your advice and all.

BUSH: What advice? This is the first I've heard from you since 1992. I kept phoning the White House about a putter I'd left behind and nobody would take my call.

CARTER: If I endorse you, can I go to Rwanda?

REAGAN: Sorry, Bill, didn't hear you. Damn hearing aid must be on the fritz again.

FORD: Endorsement? Like on a check?

Isn't it fascinating to hear men who have made history, talking about it in their own words? And I think a point becomes obvious: Recovery has benefited so many people in the public eye that you almost begin to suspect any leader who *isn't* in recovery. How could you entrust the nation to someone who still, say, seethes and stews with the bitter memory of his war experiences, his past political failures, his lockstep support of supply side deficit-nomics, his big-butt wife and his own clock-stopping face? I'm not going to name any names—that would be too easy, like Doling out chunks of Dole pineapple instead of letting you Bob for your own—but it's worth thinking about.

RECOVERING FROM NOT INHALING

I don't see what the big deal is about my not inhaling when I tried marijuana during my college years. If you look at the record, you'll see that not inhaling was completely consistent with my behavior at that time.

You have to understand what the peer pressure was like back then. This was the height of the Vietnam era, and even though I was not dodging the draft and did not organize an antiwar protest which I did not attend, there was a great emphasis on our generation's political and cultural "solidarity." You were either "cool" or "square," and because I had a big poster of Huey Long in my room, I was already in danger of being branded the latter. I knew that if I was going to pursue a career in public service I had to reach out and touch all sectors of my generation. I needed that "cool" label.

Therefore, when my dorm buddies suggested one night that we go see a Jefferson Airplane concert, I went along, although at no point did I actually agree that it was a good idea. We stopped at a roadhouse on the way and my friends ordered up several pitchers of 3.2 beer. Mindful of the toll taken on our nation's highways by drunk drivers, I didn't swallow mine. Outside the concert a hawker was selling some really excellent "Fuck the System" T-shirts, and I bought one to support him in his effort to stay off welfare and to protect the First Amendment. I am offended by gratuitous obscenity, of course, so I didn't wear it.

Inside the concert hall the music was deafening; since I am sensitive to loud noise, this presented me with a dilemma. Fortunately, I solved it by simply not listening. But during the show someone passed me a marijuana cigarette—I believe they called them "joints"—and, wanting to appear like "one of the guys," I admit that I puffed on it. As I have previously stated, I did not inhale. Later on I was glad I hadn't dulled my senses, because we picked up some townie chicks who were looking to make it with college guys. I didn't ejaculate.

Chapter Eleven

THE OPEN PRESIDENCY

I have outlined my Twelve Steps. I have explained my Twelve Steps. Now I am ready to embark upon my Twelve Steps . . . but I realize some of you may still be feeling a little uneasy about your President opening the State of the Union Address by saying, "My name is Bill C. and I've got a problem." Therefore I would like to take this opportunity to answer some of the most frequently asked questions about presidential recovery.

Q: In Step One, you admit that you've been unable to accomplish anything in your first term. Why should we believe you can accomplish anything in a second term? Hey, you believed me once, didn't you?

Q: Why should I vote for someone in recovery when I can vote for someone not in recovery?

I don't care who you are, everybody's got a problem. The first step in solving it is to admit that it exists. A candidate who is not in recovery hasn't even taken that first step, and having someone that self-deluded in a position of power is not only a disservice to the country—it's downright dangerous.

Q: Will Mrs. Clinton be undergoing recovery as well?

Why should I? There's nothing wrong with me.

Q: I'm not sure I can support someone who doesn't take responsibility for his own actions. Sorry, you'll have to leave. This book is for people who vote in American elections.

Q: Will you have to go to meetings like people in other Twelve-Step programs?

Yes, I've already told Hillary that I will be out Monday nights at my weekly meeting down at the Sheraton.

You said it was at the Holiday Inn.

Did I? Yes, the Holiday Inn, that's right. And don't wait up—some of these people get up to tell their stories and they just go on and on and on.

Don't worry. Monday's my bowling night.

You bowl? Since when?

Oh, I joined a First Ladies' League. Thing is, the only alley time we could get was very, very late. So don't wait up.

Q: Won't the Republicans just use your being in recovery to strengthen their case against you? I'm not worried about that. I truly believe that their case against me can't get any stronger. Besides, my position is that you can't spell Republican without the first two letters of Recovery.

Q: How can you call that a position? It's completely inane. Sorry, you'll have to leave. This book is for people who vote in American elections.

Q: How will a recovered Bill Clinton govern differently from the pre-recovery Bill Clinton?

I will be more decisive. I will be more forceful. I will be more responsive. I will not be so quick to compromise my ideals. I will be less vulnerable to political considerations. I will govern with vision, strength, commitment and idealism. I will stop leaving the seat up. I will write thank-you notes within a week of receiving gifts. I will have the White House gutters and leaders flushed every fall. I will try to come up with something positive to say about Hillary's hair no matter what godawful thing she does to it. I will really cut back on the fats and give the carrot sticks another try. I will drop the *Penthouse* subscription and start reading Stephanopoulos's briefing papers. I will work on my abs. I will vacuum the floor covers in the limousine. I will look both ways before crossing. I will finally watch all those episodes of *The Simpsons* I taped. I will remember to empty my pants pockets before putting them in the hamper. I will continue my commitment to build a better, stronger America. And I will learn to snowboard.

RECOVERING FROM A LUNATIC CRASHING HIS PLANE ON YOUR FROM LAWN

When you decide to run for President, you expect to give up a certain amount of privacy. But to have your yard turn into some kind of emergency landing strip for nut cases? Do you have any idea what it's like to be standing in the bathroom in your skivvies, checking in the mirror for chancres, when all of a sudden screaming comes across the sky and this big sort of shooting flame flashes by the window and you hear a huge WHUMP and Hillary calls in from the bedroom, "Check it out, there's one less Republican vote in '96"? It's unnerving, that's what it is. The skies just aren't safe any more. And I can't help thinking that this all goes back to Reagan firing the air traffic controllers.

So what's to be done about securing White House air space? I've got an idea—the kind of progressive, *inexpensive* idea that I'll be rolling out all the time in my second term. I'm planning to build an air traffic control tower here on the White House grounds, and staff it with inner-city youths—young people that society has given up on. Our education system may have failed them, but a lot of them are pretty amazing at Super Nintendo, and after all, what does that involve? Looking at a screen and shooting. So I'll have one team of young people monitoring the radar screens for any unauthorized aircraft, and another group manning the adjacent Patriot missile installation ready to blow them to hell and back. This will improve White House security immeasurably. And since those Patriots have been known to go off course now and then, if one of them inadvertently ends up in Newt Gingrich's bedroom, well, that's the breaks, Bunky.

Chapter Twelve

A COUPLE MORE THINGS ABOUT THAT BASTARD DOLE

Did you know Dole chews with his mouth open? Yeah. Then afterward he picks his teeth. People ask me why I wasn't able to work more effectively with him in my first term.id you know Dole chews with his mouth open? Yeah. Then afterward he picks his teeth. People ask me why I wasn't able to work more effectively with him in my first term. *You* try hosting a White House breakfast for a guy who keeps flashing you peeks at his mashed-up bran muffin. Plus I saw him get a little mint jelly on his hand once and when he thought no one was looking he wiped it right on the seat of his chair. At least I *think* it was mint jelly, if you know what I mean. He borrowed Gore's pen one time and didn't give it back, and Gore moped around the place for a week. It was his Garfield pen with the winking eyes. Also, have you seen Dole's socks? He wears those cheap K Mart ones without enough elastic so when he crosses his legs you can see his shins. He has extremely ugly shins. Don't even get me started on the flatulence issue.

Bill, this chapter isn't strictly related to recovery, is it?

I guess not, but it's sure making me feel a hell of a lot better.

But, darling, do you really want to end this book with such a bitter personal attack? It's not very presidential.

No, I suppose you're right, Hillary.

I think the readers might be more interested in your thoughts and feelings as you prepare for your re-election campaign.

Good point. Now, I don't know if you think and feel the way I do when you see a severe case of dandruff, but I can tell you none of the other senators even wants to sit *near* Dole in the Chamber because they get those flakes all over their suits and they're so greasy and disgusting that the dry cleaner charges them extra . . .

RECOVERING FROM A BIG FAT NASTY DICTATOR WHO LIVES TOO DAMN CLOSE SENDING HALF HIS POPULATION OVER IN BOATS

If there's one thing I can't stand, it's people taking advantage of my good nature. You got this Castro down in Havana thinking, "Hey, this Bill Clinton guy's another Southern Democrat wussie. Let me send him a few thousand felons that we don't need anymore, just like I did with Jimmy Carter." Well, uh-uh, Fidel, mi amigo. We don't want your hardened criminals. We've got our own. So pay attention, chum. Knock it off with the refugees or I'm sending a boat *your* way. And it's not going to be some raft made out of banana stalks, either. It's going to be a twin-engine Cigarette racing shell capable of sixty knots, and on board are going to be Bob Dole, Newt Gingrich, Ross Perot, a VCR showing Rush Limbaugh videocassettes and a thermos of really strong espresso, and when those fellows land on your shore they're going to be so wired on caffeine and Rush that they'll tear you a new asshole just like they've done to me. And if you think Jimmy Carter's going to fly down there and save your ass, well, I have news for you: the whole thing was his idea. Way to go, Jimmy. Have another wine cooler, on the United States Government.

AFTERWORD:

ON A PERSONAL NOTE

My fellow Americans, by now I think it's pretty clear that I am no longer the President I was, and I am well on my way to not even being the President I am now. And that is good news for you, Mr. and Ms. American Voter. (Also for you, Mr. and Mr. American Voter and Ms. and Ms. American Voter. I'm going to really put my foot down on this gays in the military thing very very soon. And you, Master and Miss Young American Voter—don't forget who went on MTV and fielded questions about his underwear. Don't forget who had Michael Stipe and that Megadeth guy jamming at his inaugural. Don't forget who secretly helicoptered into Woodstock '94 in the dead of night to score some quick feels off the topless chicks in the crowd. Oops, I wasn't going to mention that.)

Why is it good news? Because every day, in every way, I'm getting better—and frankly, I wasn't that bad to begin with! I have spent my whole life preparing to serve America as its President, and I have a really strong feeling that I'm just about ready to commence. I have put my will and my fate in the hands of my Higher Power, and that Higher Power has turned around and said to me, "Bill, you go right back to the White House and finish what you started. And when you're done with that, get her out of there before Hillary gets back and then get the heck out on the campaign trail and get yourself reelected!" And remember, that's not me speaking, it's God!

My fellow Americans, the job you elected me to do in 1992 is *not* finished. (Neither is the job you elected me to do in 1978, 1982, 1984, 1986 and 1990, but that's another book.) The health care crisis has not been solved. The deficit crisis has not been solved. And there are still eight people in Washington who haven't served as the White House communications director. Those people deserve their chance. I deserve another chance. Stipe says he wants to play Washington again. I can't give him that opportunity unless you reelect me. Let me stay. Please. I wasn't going to mention this, but . . . this would be a really bad time for me to be out of a job. The wife has another bun in the oven.

WHAT?!?

Just play along, okay? I'm desperate here.

Have you lost your mind?

Look, I meant to tell you about this but I haven't had a minute. It's just for the polls. You said you wanted another child.

That was in 1985. What am I going to do with a baby now?

If we time this right you can get bigger and bigger through the campaign and deliver on the eve of Election Day! The voters will eat it up!

Yeah, and what happens afterward? And don't you dare tell me Stephanopoulos wants to be a nanny.

Oh, Gingrich will have his orphanages running by then. What do you say?

Don't touch me, you creep.

RECOVERING FROM LOSING YOUR
PARTY'S RENOMINATION

I suppose if you're President and you put yourself in the running for re-election and your own party goes ahead and nominates someone else, some people would interpret that as a vote of no confidence. Nonsense, say I. If such a thing were to happen to me—not that I expect it to, not in a million years, don't get me wrong—I'd merely consider it a thank-you from my fellow Democrats, their way of saying, "You did your time, Bill, you put in your years of public service, and dammit, we appreciate it. Now it's time to take the wisdom and experience you've gained, and share it with America's young people by accepting a generously endowed Chair of Governmental Studies at some Ivy League school. And while you're at it, there are several corporations who could really benefit from your presence on their board of directors. *Real* corporations, classy ones that have absolutely nothing to do with chickens."

That's what such an action would say to me. What does it say to you, Messrs. Higher Education and Corporate America?

POST-AFTERWORD:

A CONFIDENTIAL
MEMORANDUM

EYES ONLY
FROM: HR
TO: You, The Voter
RE: WJC

1996 looms large, and it doesn't look pretty. I'd like to cut through all the political doublespeak for once and address you, the voter, intelligent adult to intelligent adult. No lying, no spinning, and totally confidential, just between you and me. Bill's rooting around the White House kitchen looking for brownies left over from the state dinner for the Oak Ridge Boys. Or nailing one of the assistant cooks. Whatever.

Look, we made some mistakes. Granted. Bill Clinton's not perfect. Granted. We got into office and assumed that those things we said we were going to do—tackling big problems and asking Americans to make sacrifices, fighting off lobbyists and special interests—you really wanted us to do. Okay. It was political naivete. It won't happen again.

Listen, Bill is only forty-nine years old. I can't have this guy hanging around the house for another twenty or thirty years, okay? I've got some deals going, a lot of meetings, I've got important people coming over, and I just can't have him sitting in the living room watching *The Simpsons* in a muscle-T and boxer shorts, his stomach flopping over the waistband, wolfing down a Big Mac and asking my guests if they remember his D-Day Anniversary speech from 1994. Please reelect Bill Clinton. He's a good man, relatively speaking, and I promise I'll keep an eye on him for the next four years and make sure he doesn't try anything too ambitious. Then when we get a few more issues settled, get the money in place and the people in position, Tipper and I will announce our candidacy. And come Inauguration Day, 2001, I won't forget the people who put me in the White House. My only agenda will be to respond to *you*, the people. I'll make sure *you* get the kind of government you want, and *only afterward* will I enact sweeping social legislation, rebuild the cities, overhaul the federal government, realign the economy for the next century, and then, by God, I'm going to pass a health care bill if it takes an invasion of the Senate by the United States Marine Corps.

　　　Like I said: Government that responds to *you*. So remember: Vote for Rodham. Clinton, I mean. Vote for Clinton. Yes. Thank you and God bless you.

Test Your Political Recovery Knowledge

Have you absorbed enough from this book to effectively support the President's recovery? Take this short quiz to find out.

The reason President Clinton badly misread the public mood vis-a-vis health care reform is:
A) He was too preoccupied with defending himself against unjust personal attacks.
B) The public is wrong and stupid. And my name is Rodham, damn it.
C) He didn't misread it, God misread it to him.
D) His dog ate it.

We must not instruct our public-school children about masturbation because:
A) The subject should only be taught by experts.
B) That sort of thing is best learned at home.
C) Why spoil it for them by giving it a scientific name?
D) It should be left in God's hand. Er, hands.

The best thing about a middle-class tax cut is:
A) The whopping twenty bucks it puts in your pocket come April fifteenth.
B) The warm feeling it gives everyone but the workers who lose their jobs because of it.
C) The way it makes the deficit bounce back up to record highs so we can blame everything on *that.*
D) That it's not "politics as usual."

Which Republican proposal is most likely to suffer a Clinton veto?
A) Giving fetuses the vote
B) Mandatory execution of illegal aliens
C) Nationwide conversion of universities into prisons
D) Compulsory Bible readings during sex

*Bill Clinton has been called a President "in the JFK mold." This
       description is based on:*
A) His charismatic personality.
B) His youthful exuberance for life.
C) His vision for America's future.
D) The Cuban Missile Crisis in his pants.

*Logic: If we posit that Bill Clinton is a great thinker, we may therefore
       infer that the expression "food for thought" refers to:*
A) Fried mozzarella sticks.
B) Corn dogs.
C) Cheese-flavored popcorn.
D) The jumbo box of two dozen foil-wrapped Ho-Ho's.
E) All of the above, washed down with a Big Gulp.

Bill Clinton is considered "a man of the people" because:
A) He has slept with half of them.
B) Underneath the Yale and Oxford education, he's the same
       dependable white trash he always was.
C) He sure as hell isn't a man of the hour or a man of destiny, so
       "the people" is the only thing left.
D) Men of the people who need people are the luckiest people
       in the world.

Bill Clinton deserves a second term because:
A) He needs another four years to put America on the road to a
       healthy twenty-first century.
B) He never attempted to undermine the Constitution, sell off
       the national forests to developers, trade arms for hostages
       or start a war to boost his popularity ratings.
C) He sublet his place in Arkansas and the lease runs another
       five years.
D) He hasn't suffered enough.

Complete the following sentences:
"This woman's claims are totally_____"
"This trooper's claims are totally_____"
"This chicken's claims are totally_____"

"Don't ask, don't tell" refers to the White House policy on:
A) Homosexuals in the military.
B) Arkansas real estate deals.
C) Who will pay for health care reform.
D) Stuckey's waitresses.

True or False:
• "Stephanopoulos" is an anagram for "Poo, house plant."
• A "Middle Class Bill of Rights" is really, really different from a "Contract With America."
• Newt Gingrich believes a single word of what he's saying.

The Republican Party proposes to solve the problems of poverty, illegitimate births, crime and the federal deficit by:
A) prayer.
B) worship.
C) supplication.
D) beseeching the Lord.

Complete the following sentences:
1) "This is an outrageous lie. I met the woman briefly at a political function in 1988 and at no time did I offer to massage her_____"
2) "This is preposterous. No governor in his right mind would attempt_____with *one* woman in the back of a highway patrol cruiser, let alone three."

Hillary Clinton and Barbara Bush:
Compare and Contrast

Hillary Clinton is to Barbara Bush as:
A) David Caruso is to Dennis Franz.
B) A Chihuahua is to a Shar-pei.
C) Randy "Macho Man" Savage is to "King Kong" Bundy.
D) A lemon is to a prune.

*The main difference between Hillary Clinton and Barbara Bush is
        one of:*
A) Personal style.
B) Political philosophy.
C) Familial priorities.
D) Collagen.

Essay Question:

Please state *in your own words* (75 words or less) why Ross Perot
should not be running around loose.

Scoring:

80-100 You have been listening carefully to Stephanopoulos during
staff meetings. You are the only one. **60-80** You read the newspaper
carefully every day, and yet for some reason you still haven't taken your
own life. **40-60** You are a member of the United States Congress. **0-40**
You are hopelessly stupid, your wife is very unpleasant and you *still* don't
know how to spell "potato."

Beautiful Civil Servants
Are Waiting to,
Talk to, You now!

Call 1-900-555-ELVI For a Progress Report on
the President's Recovery!

President William Jefferson Clinton is in the fight of his life—the fight to regain political credibility in time for the 1996 presidential election. Can he do it in time? Can he do it at all? Would he rather be somewhere else, just plain doing it? Now you can get an up-to-the-second progress report on the President's recovery, any time day or night, by calling the White House Party Line!

When you call the White House Party Line at 1-900-555-ELVI ("Leave off the S for Second Term!"), *you* choose the type of presidential aide you wish to speak with—blonde, brunette, ethnic, chubby, kinky—for only $9.95 for the first three minutes, $2.00 per each additional minute. Your presidential aide will update you on the President's recovery, as well as such issues as economic stimulus initiatives, foreign trade treaty reforms, deficit reduction packages, and what she'd do to you with her tongue if she could get you alone and naked right there with her in the East Wing. All revenues collected go into a blind trust[*] for retired Presidents from Arkansas.

Don't be left "in the dark" about the President's recovery—at least, not without a beautiful phone friend there in the dark with you! **Call the White House Party Line today!**

---

[*] Standard brokerage account administered by a blind investment banker under the supervision of Hillary Rodham Clinton.

This is not a real advertisement for a real service. It's a fake advertisement for a fake service. It was placed here for your amusement. These little footnotes were placed here for the amusement of your family and friends, who think you look really funny when you squint.

For sales, editorial information, subsidiary rights information
or a catalog, please write or phone or e-mail

iBooks
1230 Park Avenue
New York, New York 10128
Sales: 1-800-68-BRICK
Tel: 212-427-7139
www.ibooksinc.com
bricktower@aol.com

For sales in the UK and Europe please contact our distributor,
Gazelle Book Services
White Cross Mills
Lancaster, LA1 4XS, UK
Tel: (01524) 68765 Fax: (01524) 63232
email: jacky@gazellebooks.co.uk

www.ingramcontent.com/pod-product-compliance
Lightning Source LLC
La Vergne TN
LVHW051352080426
835509LV00020BB/3395